Nantucket Ghosts

Nantucket Ghosts

44 True Accounts

by Blue Balliett

Photographs by Lucy Bixby

Down East Books
Camden, Maine

10-digit ISBN 0-89272-717-9
13-digit ISBN 978-0-89272-717-9

Printed at Versa Press, Inc., East Peoria, Illinois

4   3

Down East Books
Camden, Maine
A division of Down East Enterprise
Distributed to the trade by National Book Network, Inc.
Book Orders: 800-685-7962
www.downeastbooks.com

Library of Congress Control Number: 2006926810

Table of Contents

Introduction

Nantucket Island has just over 10,000 year-round residents—and a sizeable population of ghosts.

The forty-four stories in this book were collected as oral history over a fifteen-year period, and originally published in two volumes: *The Ghosts of Nantucket* (1984) and *Nantucket Hauntings* (1990). These interviews are direct, unembellished accounts—experiences related to me in living rooms, on back porches, sometimes outside so as not to be heard by the house itself. In recording these tales, I tried not to believe or disbelieve, but simply to get out of the way.

Among those who speak are a janitor, an electrician, a museum curator, two architects, a carpenter, a writer, a marine biologist, a chef, a nurse, a jeweler, several guesthouse owners, a taxi driver, a real estate agent, a teacher, a hairdresser, an antiques dealer, and a restaurant owner. The youngest is seven and the oldest ninety-three; some of their names have been changed at their request. A few are Nantucketers, most are off-Islanders, and all, interestingly enough, saw themselves as unlikely candidates for the sort of experience that happened to them.

A plump comma of land twenty-two miles off the south shore of Cape Cod in Massachusetts, Nantucket has managed to punctuate the history of the United States in a way that is out of all proportion to its diminutive size. Seventeen miles long from east to west and three to four miles wide, the island was one of the most prosperous whaling ports in the world during the first half of the nineteenth century, and produced an impressive number of politicians, philosophers, abolitionists, suffragettes, inventors, writers, and scientists. With the collapse of the whaling industry, however, Nantucket became an impoverished, deserted outpost.

In the early 1900s, city dwellers began to discover this tiny backwater. As a retreat from mainstream American life, Nantucket seemed too good to be true. It has seventy miles of beach, fields of berries and wildflowers, slow summers, and winding, narrow streets banked by Quaker homes. It was back on the map.

The physical remnants of Nantucket's bustling heyday stood unchanged; the decline of the whaling industry and the severe depression that followed had the effect of freezing almost all housing construction for more than half a century. The town, through an accident of history, has one of the most extensive and remarkably preserved collections of pre-1850 buildings in the United States. The soft, gray coloring of shingled houses dominates the landscape.

Of the people I interviewed in gathering these stories, many did not know that paranormal disturbances are quite common on the island, and they were initially reluctant or embarrassed to speak about their experience. Most prefaced their story with a phrase like, "Well, this sounds ridiculous, but . . ." Others admitted over the phone that "certain things" had gone on in their homes, but were unwilling to talk about them.

In listening to these accounts, I often felt like pinching myself; how *could* I be hearing what I was hearing? How could so many "real" ghosts be coming out of a modern community? Nantucket's cache of well-preserved old houses must be a factor; moisture offers another explanation. The late Arthur Twitchell, a former president of the American Society for Psychical Research, had an interesting theory. He felt that the perception of an apparition was an electrical process not yet understood in scientific terms, a process possibly facilitated on Nantucket by the constant presence of water in the ground and the atmosphere. The island's aquifer sits very close to the surface, and Nantucket's fogs are notorious. There are coastal regions in Great Britain that are similar in climate and terrain to this island, and Twitchell pointed out that some of the communities in those areas of Great Britain also report a bumper crop of phantoms and hobgoblins.

Nantucket has always been a difficult and isolated spot. It is also a place of great beauty. Both frustrating and moving in its limitations, it is a corner of the world that is hard to leave or forget; perhaps that is as good an explanation as any for the existence of a very real population of ghosts.

I would like to thank all those who kindly invited me into their lives so many years ago and took the time to share the experiences that appear in this book. The privilege of listening to their stories is still with me.

I also want to thank Lucy Bixby, whose photographs add a wonderful new dimension to these accounts. These elegant images go far beyond illustration—they truly capture something of the soul of Nantucket.

Special thanks also go to the Nantucket Historical Association, which owns several of the properties Lucy photographed. Lucy tells me they were terrific about unlocking doors and providing access, and needed no convincing on the subject of ghosts.

Blue Balliett
Chicago, 2006

The Abbess

"This is about a very solid ghost. Even though it's been—oh, Lord— almost fifty years, I'd know her if I met her today."

Natalie Orloff, the kind of person who manages to look active even when supine, was curled up on the sofa in her bathing suit. The house she owns with her husband, Louis, is on the Bluff, a steep cliff rising above the ocean at 'Sconset. She is a rapid and confident talker. She gestured with her cigarette toward the window, beyond which the Sankaty lighthouse loomed in the west.

"It is that gray house across the hedge there. That's where she's been seen. My parents bought the house in 1923 or '24. It had been empty during World War I, and was used by rumrunners during Prohibition. It was completely vandalized. There was a hole in the roof from a fire that someone had built in the middle of the living room. Not one piece of china or glass was intact. I was four or five when we got it, and I remember that Mother wouldn't let me walk on the floors when we went to see it. We had to climb through a window to get in, as the front door was busted. I was in Mother's arms, and she and Dad were ankle-deep in broken glass and garbage.

"Mother was wild about the location, which was the reason they bought it. Dad was planning to tear down the house and build another until he found out that the basic structure was worth a hefty $8,000. As he had only paid $1,400 for the house and land, they decided to keep the original house. It was remodeled, and new wings were added.

"Mother turned it into a beautiful, unlivable house. She had painted floors, which showed every grain of sand, and twenty-three flower vases downstairs.

I remember the number because I had to change the water in them every morning.

"My bedroom was next to Mother's at the top of a flight of stairs. Dad's was around the corner and down the hall. The light from Sankaty Head flooded my room at night, and when I couldn't sleep, I counted the beams running across the ceiling. We were practically under the lighthouse, as you can see. That's an important detail, for it meant that when I opened my bedroom door at night, the light flooded the stairwell also.

"One night when I was seven or eight, I heard the sound of heavy footsteps on the stairs. I was in bed, and so was Mother, but we both got up and opened our doors. Dad was in his room, but I think we both wondered if it were him, and wanted to see if anything was wrong. There, coming up the stairs, was a very pleasant-looking nun with a pug nose and a round face. She must have weighed a hundred and sixty pounds if she weighed an ounce. We were both too surprised to move, but I don't remember feeling particularly scared. She wasn't in the least bit like a ghost, and I don't think the thought even crossed my mind until several minutes later. She had a self-assured, friendly air. Her skirts practically brushed us as she turned the corner at the top of the stairs and started down the hall to Dad's room. Now, Dad was simply not the kind of man you would just walk in on or startle, and at that point Mother came to her senses. She blurted out, 'Oh, you can't go in *there*!' The nun paused before Dad's door, gave us a warm, broad smile, and disappeared. Dad knew nothing about this whole business the next morning, and he never did see the Abbess, as we came to call her.

"Mother began to look into the history of the house. She found out that it had been built in about 1870 by two sisters who were devout Catholics. Their name was Corbett. They were very close, and when one of them died, around 1900, the other left Nantucket and loaned the house to a Boston convent as a retreat. The nuns had the property up until the First World War, when travel costs and supply shortages probably made the house too expensive to use. Some of the islanders my mother talked to said that they remembered seeing nuns down on the beach at 'Sconset. I guess the nuns were considered something of an oddity. She also found out, by describing the woman we saw that night to a neighbor, that she was dressed as a mother superior.

"I have never had the shadow of a doubt about having seen the Abbess. She had such an amiable air that it was the fact that she was a phenomenon I didn't understand, and one that my parents obviously didn't either, that terrified me. She looked as solid as anyone I'd ever known, and a good deal nicer than many.

"My mother saw her on several occasions, and I saw her once more. I was twelve at the time, and had a friend staying for the night. The two of us were sleeping in the big bed in my father's room. We woke up in the night to see the Abbess standing at the foot of the bed, smiling down at us. Predictably, we started in on preadolescent shrieks and giggles, and dove under the sheets. By the time we stuck our heads out, she was gone.

"When I was in my teens, I would often come downstairs to find a date, who had been waiting politely in the living room, looking dazed. In fact, he would be paralyzed. The problem was usually that he had been watching objects move independently around the room. A picture would be straightened, an ashtray centered on a table, or a bouquet ruffled—and always by an unseen hand. I have to admit, when I was dropped off by my date late at night, I got very good at zooming up the stairs in no time flat. I could have made some track records. The thought of meeting the Abbess in the dark wasn't appealing.

"I had one more experience with the Abbess—or at least, I think it was she; I never actually saw who it was. One evening in 1947, my friend Marjorie Benchley and I were having a drink alone together in the house. We hadn't seen each other for five or six years because of the war. We were chatting about personal things when someone came into the room and sat down on a chair. Now, we couldn't see anything, and the cushions weren't depressed, but there was no question about it. We both knew from looking at each other that we were feeling the same thing. We couldn't remember anything that we really wanted to discuss, so we made ridiculous small talk for about half an hour, hoping that whoever had seemingly joined us would leave.

"Finally, the situation became unbearable, and I said to Marj, 'Don't you think we need another drink?' She came into the kitchen with me, and after a whispered consultation, we decided to go back and wait it out. We took our drinks back into the living room. Whoever had been with us was still there. About twenty minutes later, this presence got up and walked out of the room. I can't tell you how we both knew precisely when it came and went, for I have no idea, but the closest I can get to describing that feeling is by telling you to imagine someone coming quietly into a room where you're sitting alone reading. Before anything has been said, you know that someone is in the room. Your senses seem to be telling you that there's another person near. It's a familiar feeling, probably just some form of convenient animal radar.

"That was the last experience I had with the Abbess before we sold the house in 1950. Mother had one kind of taste and I had another; I wasn't about to run around all summer sweeping up after sandy feet. So now Louis and I have this house next door. I'd love to ask the present owners of the house whether they've ever seen the Abbess, but I don't want to scare them. People have funny reactions to these things.

"This is just an aside, but I had one other experience with a ghost on Nantucket. In 1945, I was renting a little cottage in 'Sconset called the Brig. My husband was away most of the summer, so I was alone with my five-year-old son. I would be busy doing something in the house, and would suddenly get the feeling that someone was watching me. There, outside one of the ground-floor windows, would be a sharp-faced little old lady. I saw her a number of times, always in broad daylight. She was absolutely solid. Her clothes were dark and unfamiliar to me, and she always had a bonnet on. I don't remember if it was in the Quaker style; I just remember the bonnet strings under her chin. As soon as we would catch each other's eyes, she would dart away, moving much faster than was humanly possible, and vanish. Something about her expression made me think of a shy person who was snooping, and I would almost feel embarrassed to 'catch' her looking in. I saw her inside only once. I walked into the living room in mid-afternoon, and she was sitting in a chair. Again, she was a three-dimensional, seemingly living figure, and there was nothing misty or ghostlike about her body. She gave me a quick, defiant look, then—*pffft!*—she disappeared. She was there one moment and simply not the next. When I looked at the empty chair, the cushions were still puffed up.

"But that's another experience. This island, as I'm sure you know, is loaded with ghosts. If someone like me has seen them, they have to be all over."

Mr. and Mrs. Julius Jensen bought the house from the Orloffs. Mr. Jensen's mother, who is no longer alive, saw the Abbess in the early 1950s. His mother, he said, was not the kind of person to imagine things. She had been a frontier nurse, and was an exceptionally fearless character.

Mr. Jensen's mother had seen a large, heavy woman in a nun's habit on the stair landing. She wasn't able to make out the features of the face, for the head was draped with a loose, shroudlike piece of material. The figure seemed to be giving off very cold air.

Mr. Jensen had listened with interest to his mother's experience, but didn't think much of it; she was getting rather old. And he had never, until his conversations with me, heard about Mrs. Orloff's tales of the Abbess.

Makaala and Liz Wolven spent a winter in the house in the late 1960s. They had three dogs at the time. Mrs. Wolven said that she liked the house, but that her dogs were never comfortable there. She and her husband knew nothing about the Abbess.

The dogs refused to go into the bedroom at the head of the stairs. To conserve heat, the Wolvens generally kept the upstairs doors tightly shut, but when they would return after being out, the door and one window in this room would always be open. Mrs. Wolven said that the dogs had an infuriating number of accidents in that house, and never wanted to stay there alone.

Mrs. Wolven mentioned that she and her husband would sometimes have the strange feeling of being watched by someone in the stairwell or in that problematic bedroom. They did their best to ignore this sensation.

The Abbess was last seen in the early 1970s. A young couple who were renting the house looked out the window one stormy day in January to see a nun standing on the front lawn in full regalia, her habit billowing and snapping in the wind. They were puzzled at this strange sight, but when she vanished into thin air they were petrified. Not knowing what else to do, they called the police. The officer at the desk put them in touch with Nathaniel Benchley, then living year-round on Nantucket. Mr. Benchley and his wife Marjorie had spent many summers in 'Sconset, and he was able to explain the story of the house to them. Unfortunately, he was unable, years later, to remember their name.

The Shimmering Bubble

The 1800 House on Mill Street is located in an old section of the town. The house has no sidewalk in front, and sits, plain and stiff-backed, on a little rise a couple of feet from the macadam. It has a rough fieldstone foundation and a steep flight of stairs which rise sharply to the front door.

The building gives off a feeling of separateness that is not welcoming. Many of Nantucket's historic houses seem graciously openhearted in their old age, but the 1800 House just doesn't. It is alive with the arthritic sounds of old wood; pops, ticks, and creaks are audible in every room. The building was restored by the Nantucket Historical Association in the early '50s and is an early example of a form of construction popular on Nantucket in the first half of the nineteenth century. A central door with two equidistant windows on either side added a certain formality that the earlier lean-to houses never had. One opens the front door into a small stair hall leading into parlors on the left and on the right. The effect is like that of holding a stick in a rapid stream; the stairs shoot upward from the front hall, and the passage forks around the stairwell, meeting again in the large keeping room. The keeping room, where most of the cooking and living was once done, has five doors: one on either side of the fireplace, opening into each of the front parlors, one to a borning room on the west, one to a weaving room on the east, and one to a summer kitchen in back. The door that plays a part in this story is the parlor door on the west end of the keeping room, near the door to the borning room.

Nineteenth-century families spent most of their winter months in the keeping room. With its large hearth and southern exposure, it must have been the warmest and most welcoming room in the house. The borning room was used for just that purpose. Not much bigger than a cubbyhole, it was easy to keep warm in the winter, and was convenient not only for giving birth but for taking care of sick children or the elderly. There are five large rooms upstairs.

In midwinter of 1972, electrician Parker Gray was hired to install a complex alarm system in the building. The alarm system consisted of infrared and ultrasonic rays, backed up with magnetic contacts fastened onto all of the doors and windows. When the system is on, an alarm goes off in the police station if a window or door is opened, or if any solid object passes through the infrared or ultrasonic beams.

From the time it was first activated, the alarm went off between seven and quarter to eight every Tuesday and Thursday night. Each time the police hurried to the house they found it quiet and undisturbed, with the exception of the ground-floor latch door connecting the west parlor and the keeping room. This door, which was wired with magnetic contacts, would be found open.

As the electrician, Parker Gray was in an awkward position. By the fifth week of false alarms, the police and the Historical Association began to wonder if someone was playing an ingenious trick, or if Parker had indeed installed the alarm system properly. No one could think of a plausible explanation. Parker disconnected the magnetic contact so that no alarm would go off. The door would still be open on Wednesday and Friday mornings. The other four doors leading out of the keeping room were all wired to the alarm system, and all remained closed.

Parker was understandably upset by this inexplicable problem. He wondered at first if a passing truck (very unlikely on Mill Street in midwinter) or an airplane could be jiggling the door latch loose. He tried walking heavily and then jumping up and down on either side of the door to see if the latch would bounce free. No luck. The latch itself was set in a cradle nearly a half-inch deep, a type of fitting that is really too secure to be jolted open by a vibration. The only reasonable conclusion was that the latch was actually being lifted.

The possibility of a ghost in the house was not mentioned. Everyone concerned had heard about "presences" in various Nantucket homes, but no one wanted to admit the existence of a ghost that opened doors. As a last resort, Parker took his assistant to the house between 6:30 and quarter to seven one Tuesday night, and they turned off the alarm, entered quietly, and stood out of sight of the troublesome door in a small storage closet around the corner from the west parlor. The door to the storage room was left open.

They waited there for half an hour or so. Parker's assistant was just whispering to him that this was a "helluva way to spend a cold February night" when they heard the latch click. Parker, in recounting the story, said that he wanted to roar at the way his skeptical assistant blanched and rushed out the front door, slamming it behind him. Parker could hear his boots thumping off at a run down the quiet street; the man didn't even wait outside in the company truck.

When no further sounds came from the next room, Parker stepped out of the storage room and peered around the doorway leading into the west parlor. The door to the keeping room had indeed swung open, and he saw ("it seemed like an eternity, although it was probably only fifteen to thirty seconds") something moving slowly toward him. As he put it, "There was definitely something there," coming through the open door, and it wasn't a sight he had ever seen before. He described it as looking like a shimmering soap bubble the size of a basketball; it was pulsing, moving gently in and out in all directions. He used his hands to show me its shape, and said that it was about as translucent as light wax paper. It floated past him, through the west parlor door, within one or two feet of where he was standing. He could feel an "extraordinary and really horrible coldness" that seemed to surround the bubble. He said that he felt nervous but for some reason not really scared by the approach of this strange "object," for it was traveling through the west parlor in an unhurried, undeliberate way that didn't seem to have anything to do with his presence. In retrospect, he says, he doesn't know why he was so sure of this, or why he was so relaxed about standing in the path of this bizarre thing. Moving evenly at the pace of a slow walk, the bubble went past the storage closet and through the front hall and disappeared up the stairs. Parker did not follow it.

He told his story to the president of the Historical Association, and together they decided to fasten the door with an eyehook the following day. The hook and eye were attached to the west-parlor side of the door, thus preventing one from opening the door from inside the keeping room. There has been no trouble since.

The house has changed hands only five times since 1807. Shortly before the house was built, the area was described in local records as "a tract of land in the Richard Gardner share westward of Stephen Chase's house." The house first appeared on record in a deed dated February 1807, when a housewright by the name of Richard Coleman sold the homestead to Jeremiah Lawrence, "High Sheriff for the County" and a prominent official of his day. The house was probably built shortly after Coleman bought the land in 1801.

In 1856 Jeremiah's widow, Eunice, sold the house to Love Calder; James Monroe Bunker (schoolteacher, notary public, and civil engineer) bought the house in 1865 and lived there with his family for thirty-eight years, selling it to Leonora E. James in 1903. Mrs. James, a peppery and outspoken member of the community, lived in the house for forty-eight years, many of them spent with her husband and children, and sold the house to Louise Anderson Melhado in 1951. Mrs. Melhado gave it to the Historical Association shortly after she bought it, and the house is open to the public during the summer months.

Unfortunately, little is known of the Lawrence or Bunker families. Nor did Mrs. James leave behind any diaries or papers that might have shed light on the existence of the mysterious bubble. Each of the three families spent close to half a century in the building; perhaps one of the former owners is still, in spirit, making the nightly rounds.

Something Evil in the Attic

"The house is on Cliff Road. I don't feel you should use our name, but I'll tell you the story.

"My husband and I bought the house in 1960. It wasn't old; it was built in the '20s, and had been owned by only one family. The man who built it and lived there for all those years was no longer alive when we bought it, but we don't know of anything terrible ever having happened in the place.

"It all began with something our ten-year-old daughter, Janet, either imagined or saw. Her bedroom was upstairs, opposite the door to the attic. The children spent hours playing in the attic. It was their territory, a place where they set up forts and clubs and arranged things the way they wanted them.

"Janet was a little afraid of that door at night; she was a sensitive, imaginative child who had awful nightmares for years, and was very scared of the dark. She had outgrown most of those fears by the time she was nine or ten, but if anyone were to be scared by a ghost, it would certainly be she. As she tells it, she was reading in bed one night and looked up to see the attic door, which was always closed at bedtime, wide open. A shimmery, insubstantial figure of a man was standing in the doorway. Janet was petrified, and must have looked it. She says she isn't too clear about what happened next, but the figure communicated to her, either silently or in words, 'Please don't worry. Don't be scared. I don't mind if you can't look at me.' The apparition calmed Janet by letting her know that he wasn't bad and wasn't going to hurt her. He told her that his name was George. I gather that they sort of made friends.

"Now, Janet is the first to say that she may very well have imagined this entire experience. She wasn't asleep, however, and remembers the feeling of

George's presence, the feeling of losing her fear of him and of realizing he was a kind person. (George, incidentally, was not the name of the man who had owned the house before us.) She may have told the other children about this strange man the next day, but she didn't mention him to me or her father for some time. When she did, it came up casually in a conversation as something curious that she had seen one night. She was no longer spooked by him at all.

"That was the only time she saw the apparition. About four years later we had a bad fire in the attic. One of the children had left a light burning too close to the wall, and the dry wood went up in flames. Fortunately, we were home at the time, and the damage was minimal compared to what it might have been.

"After the fire, the attic needed extensive repair work, and my husband and I decided to turn it into a master bedroom. The children didn't mind, for they had more or less outgrown it as a play space. We fixed it up and began using it ourselves. That was when the trouble began.

"I was up there one day and suddenly felt something extremely frightening coming over me. I can't be precise about it, for I still don't have the faintest idea what it was. It pressed toward me and literally paralyzed me with fear. I couldn't move or talk or call out for help. It was as if it was trying to suffocate me, take me over, pull me out of my body; I really didn't know whether I could survive it that first time. It was invisible and silent. When I got my voice back I let out what I guess was a strangled-sounding squawk. I was very badly shaken.

"I've heard a number of ghost stories about Nantucket homes, but I've never heard of anything this bad occurring in any other house on the island. I don't know if one would even call this a ghost; I could only think of it as an utterly terrifying, malevolent force.

"I had a number of these attacks in our bedroom over the next few years. One even happened when my husband was in the room with me and wasn't aware that it was going on until I had broken out of it. I'm not at all the type of person to have mediumistic or otherworldly feelings; my husband, too, was scared and worried by these invisible assaults. We didn't move out of the bedroom, although perhaps we should have. We did, however, talk about selling the house.

"One of my greatest fears was that this force would try to harm one of our children or someone visiting us. Our son Paul's fiancée did have an experience very similar to mine one night. This was the only time that something happened to someone other than me, and the only time it happened outside of our attic bedroom.

"Paul and Emily were sitting downstairs after the rest of us had gone up. I remember that when I tried to put the garbage out that night after dinner I found that the back door wouldn't open. Both my son and my husband tried to free it, with no success. We had never had this problem before, but we didn't think much of it and went to bed, leaving Emily and Paul alone.

"It was close to midnight when they heard the back door open. After a short pause, they heard someone in heavy boots crossing the kitchen. Both were startled and looked toward the door. There was no one there. The footsteps continued to move at a thudding, deliberate pace, straight toward where they were sitting in the living room. They didn't have much time to react, and I guess neither moved. The steps walked right up to Emily. She was then utterly overwhelmed in a way that sounded very similar to my experiences. Paul tried to help her, sitting by her for over an hour before she came out of it. She was paralyzed, frozen by this consuming, terrifying pressure. She was extremely upset, and I remember her saying the next morning that she didn't think she could stay on in the house.

"The tide turned with something quite funny. I came to open up the house one summer with a Bulgarian woman who was going to be working for us. She was a cheery, salt-of-the-earth sort of person. We had brought along the family dog, a toy beagle terrier. From downstairs in the kitchen, I whistled to the dog, for I had put out his food. He didn't come and didn't come. I looked around, calling his name, and then heard whimpering coming from upstairs. I found the dog just inside the open door to our bedroom. He was whining and prancing in front of something that was blocking the doorway and wouldn't let him get by. I couldn't see anything, but after my own experiences, I was scared to reach into the room. I was standing in the hall wondering what on earth to do, when our housekeeper came up behind me. My heart sank, for I was afraid that once she found out there was something bad in the house, she would quit on the spot. But all she said was 'Ghost, huh?' and turning her back to the open door, gave whatever was blocking it a great bump with her fanny. She stepped in, scooped up the dog, and brought him downstairs for his supper. It didn't faze her in the least.

"That taught me something. I was sitting in our bedroom at my desk one day when I heard a pop. It was the rod holding the curtains on one window. The curtains fell to the floor. A couple of seconds later there was another pop, and then another. By then, three curtains were down. Remembering our house-keeper's attitude, I said out loud, 'All right, so I need some new curtains! Fine!' With that, all of the other curtains were ripped off and thrown to the floor. The fabric was old and faded in places, and it was indeed time to replace the cur-tains, so the next day I bought some Liberty print at Nantucket Looms and made new panels. And strangely enough, ever since then I've had the feeling that the malevolent spirit, presence, or whatever, is gone from the house.

"I guess it's possible that George, Janet's supposed apparition, felt that the attic was his territory and was trying to chase us out by attacking me. But George had seemed quite harmless and friendly, and I felt that whatever went after Emily and me was really evil. Those moments of terror were far worse than anything else I have ever known."

Heaven Is Two Weeks Away

"Powell. We're talking about Jason Powell," Mark Schofield said, crossing his legs and settling back in his chair. Mark's wife, Grace, poured three glasses of lemonade. He continued, "My former wife bought our house on Bloom Street from Jason Powell, who was a psychiatrist in New York City. I have a landscaping business, and worked for him for ten years before he sold the house. He was a good man, but he had a difficult marriage and an unlucky wife, and he loved his gin. He moved off-island for good several years ago, and had a serious hip operation. He was mixing his booze with painkillers, I guess, and he died in his sleep. No one knew the circumstances. He was alone at the time."

Mr. Schofield's comfortably creased face is accented by his eyes, which are an authoritative, almost audible blue.

"About a week after Powell died, I was awakened at three A.M. We keep a night-light in the bathroom adjacent to our bedroom, and by its light I could see someone in a long granny nightgown walking by the bed toward the bathroom. I automatically stretched my foot out to check for Grace. She was fast asleep next to me. I hate the dark, and snapped the light on in a hurry. Whatever it was disappeared. It wasn't until some time later that I remembered that Powell used to wear those old-fashioned flannel nightshirts in the winter. The next night, at the same time, I was awakened again. I felt my face lifted up and turned toward the ceiling, and there was Jason's face above me. He was smiling, as if to reassure me. I was terrified, and turned on the light and woke Grace up. Again, there was nothing there.

"The third night, I was woken up again at three A.M., this time by a loud thumping in the bathroom. Grace was still asleep. I listened for a while, then got myself together, went to the bathroom, and slowly opened the door. As I snapped on the light the noise stopped and a cold wind poured past me out the door. The window had been shut all night and was still tightly closed. I have to admit I was scared; I had never had an experience like that before.

"This next part sounds funny, but I didn't know what else to do. In the morning, I went all through the house talking to Jason. 'You old bastard,' I said, 'I know you're here and I know you're not happy with what's going on.' You see, we were friends, and I know he loved life and didn't mean to kill himself. Many people thought it was a suicide, but I'm sure it was not. As I see it, I might have been a kind of interpreter for him. He was tormented, I think, by the way he had died, and needed to get in touch with someone who was his friend. At any rate, I walked all through the house, just talking to him, and he never came back.

"I've thought about that experience a lot since then. It relieved me in a way; no matter what anyone says, I now have no doubt about a world beyond. When you talk about ghosts, you're dealing with a side of life that isn't scientific or logical—but then, dying and disappearing for good doesn't seem very logical either. When my first wife died, many years ago, I remember feeling that she was back in the house with me, for about a week after she died. Another week later, I was just as sure she was gone to wherever you do go. Powell also made his appearance within two weeks after his death. There seems to be a transition period. It's as if heaven is two weeks away."

Seth

The Unitarian Church on Orange Street was built in 1809 as the Second Congregational Meeting House Society Church. Its bell was brought from Lisbon, Portugal, in 1812 by Captain Thomas Cary. The tower has seen three clocks: the first was installed at the time of construction, the second in 1823, and the present one in 1881. In 1884, the interior was modernized by the architect F. B. Coleman, who set in the tall, elegant side windows, and added a vestry and kitchen downstairs. The *trompe l'oeil* wall painting is attributed to Carl Wendte, an artist who had previously decorated the Treasury Building in Washington.

The church has a cheerful, proud, shingled countenance. Its classical structure brings to mind the child's game, "Here is the church, here is the steeple, open the doors . . ." The famous steeple, located on the front of the building, is a landmark visible from five miles at sea. The bell, now electric, strikes every hour around the clock, with an additional fifty-two strokes for reveille at 7:00 A.M., for lunch at noon, and for curfew at 9:00 P.M.

Francis and Ellen Morgan are the janitor and housekeeper for the church. Mr. Morgan, at work in the church one morning, related the following story:

"I was in here alone one winter day six or seven years ago, and was working around in the vestry when two kids I knew tapped on the window over there, wanting to come in. It was a cold, blustery day, with snow outside, kind of nasty, so I let them in. I was in the kitchen, where I keep all my tools and such, and I could hear the kids upstairs runnin' and hootin' and dashin' back and forth the way kids do, and then I heard them clattering down the stairs and running out the front door. It slammed shut. Five or ten minutes later they were back tappin' on the window. When I let them back in, I asked, 'Why'd you go out? You knew the door was locked from outside.' And they said, 'Why, a man upstairs chased us out; he didn't want us up there, and scared us.' I knew there was no one upstairs, but I didn't say anything to the kids, not wanting to really frighten them. I think Seth, as we call the spirit in this church, has an aversion to kids gettin' into deviltry. It's not really surprising, for in the old days most folks were very rigid about those things, and people—especially children, who were supposed to be mindful of their elders—were expected to adhere to certain codes of behavior. This spirit probably disapproves of someone runnin' and shriekin' around in the House of God.

"A couple of months after that, when it was a little warmer out, I brought my young grandson here one day. I took him up to the altar to show him where our minister stands, and he wanted to know if the big Bible there was God's book, and if the seat was God's seat. My grandson was asking all sorts of regular little-boy questions. Then suddenly he got very quiet and just kept starin' at the pulpit. He said, 'I don't like that man. I don't like the way he looks.' Knowing we were alone in the church, I said, 'What man?' He pointed to the pulpit. I couldn't see anything, but I didn't tell him that, and we just went and did something else.

"Of course, you know about what happened with Cathy Cronin. When she was still teaching in Rhode Island, before she got her school under way here, she needed a quiet place to correct students' papers. She used to come work in the vestry, sittin' over by the windows in the brightest part of the room. One day when she got through, and was going home along the pathway outside, she heard a terrific bang against one of those windows, and looking up saw a bodiless hand waving—in a flat arc from left to right—good-bye to her.

"One morning I was working in the vestry when I heard a really hard bang on one of the windows over there. This had happened to me twice before. If someone had actually gone up to the window and hit it that hard, I'm sure the blow would have driven the sash out and smashed the glass. So I said out loud, "Now, be careful, or you'll break it." It hasn't happened again.

"Susie Jarrell, the organist, often comes in here alone, and she has said she's heard things in the organ loft upstairs. Once when she was downstairs practicing in the vestry, she felt something pullin' her toward the corner over there, near the windows. She kept looking over, but didn't see anything. I know just what kind of feeling she's talking about; there are times when I'm in here cleaning or puttering around, and just know I'm not alone. You can feel a definite presence.

"Ted Anderson, our minister, came to the church in 1972. After he'd been here a short while, we told him that there was a spirit in the building. He laughed, at the time. But one evening shortly after his arrival here, he was upstairs alone, just strolling back and forth in the aisle, putting his sermon together, when he heard the repeated sound of a pencil dropping. He told us about it. My wife and I have heard that many times. The first time it happened to us, we were working in different parts of the building, and each thought the other was dropping something over and over. Finally she called out to me, 'Would you quit droppin' that pencil! It's makin' me irritated!' The upstairs is all carpeted, you know, up and down the aisle and between the pews. You shouldn't be hearing the sound of a pencil dropping on a bare floor when the floor's got a carpet on it!

"I think Seth is a nice spirit. It seems that he just gets a little restless sometimes, and that's when we hear him dropping things, or walking up and down the hallway in the vestry, for we often hear footsteps. We call the spirit Seth because Seth F. Swift, the first minister of the church, from 1810 to 1834, was at the helm here longer than anyone else. That's his portrait upstairs, painted by William Swain. His eyes follow you everywhere.

"About five years ago, I had an odd experience with a radio. Everything in the vestry had become mildewed over a damp winter; that spring I was scrubbing it all down and painting the ceiling. It was a tedious job. One day I brought a portable radio in with me, and had it on the platform up in front. It was tuned in to a station which played good, quiet, modern music, but then the announcer started playing this hard rock stuff. I didn't bother to change the channel. After a couple minutes of that, the radio shut right off. I went up and checked the switch, but the radio was dead as a doornail, even though it had new batteries in it. Thinking that the problem might be something in the building interfering with the reception, I walked outside with the radio, and it went right back on. But as soon as I walked back inside and set it down, it clicked right off again. I picked it up, took it outside again, and it went on. I couldn't figure out what the problem was until it occurred to me that maybe Seth didn't like the music. So I switched channels until I found a nice classical station, took the radio back inside, set it down, and it played beautifully for the rest of the day. It's a funny sensation to cross paths with a spirit when you're not expectin' it, but as I see it, Seth just has certain dislikes which he won't permit in the church, and that's when he manifests himself.

"Which reminds me—last summer we had three professional painters, brothers from Hingham, painting the outside of the church. They were steeple-jacks, too. They were almost through with the job, standing out in back takin' a rest, when the whole block-and-tackle rig on the roof came flying down and hit the ground between them. A step in the wrong direction, and one of them might have been killed. All three were astounded, and scared to death. The only way that rig could have fallen was if a person up there had loosened it. Those men do dangerous work, climbing around roofs and turrets and such, and are dependent on that rig to keep them from falling. It is always checked and rechecked, and there was absolutely no possibility, according to those men, that they could've been careless about it. They were so shaken up they could hardly eat dinner that night, and couldn't wait to get that job finished and leave Nantucket. They must have said or done something that made Seth furious.

"Some people have the misconception that spirits don't exist, but, especially on this island, they are sadly mistaken. I guess some people are scared or threatened by the idea of a ghost, but when I think about ghosts, I think about that statement made by a great leader of ours who said that 'there is nothing to fear but fear itself.' I think almost every old house here on Nantucket that's over a hundred years old has a spirit or two lingering on in it. My God, if everyone who had a ghost in their house was willin' to talk about it, you'd never get through with your project.

"My wife and I have a ghost in our house on Prospect Street. The house was built in the 1790s, and all the doors have deep latch fittings. Sometimes we'll be sittin' alone, when everything's nice and quiet, and hear the latch being opened on one of the doors, and then see the door swing open. Those aren't fastenings that can free themselves in the way a modern door can if it's not shut properly. You really have to press down on the latch to get the door open, and if the latch isn't properly dropped when you shut the door, it won't stay closed. We've also heard someone walking down the stairs from the second floor, or a chair suddenly falling over, or a door closing firmly by itself; just funny little random happenings that we had nothing to do with. We don't mind."

One Silver Spoon

"My home was built in 1746 by George Hussey as a wedding present to his daughter, Dinah, when she married Reuben Folger. In its 238 years of existence, the building has been owned by only four different families.

"I moved in thirty-one years ago and did a great deal of interior stripping, renovating, and reconstruction. It was all very exciting, for returning the house to its original condition meant getting a feeling for the people who had lived in it, too. During restoration, a roughly scrawled message was uncovered on the lintel over the keeping-room hearth. Written with chalk, using the old-fashioned *S*, it read: 'When this you see—remember me.' I've often wished I could, but there is no signature.

"Shortly after I moved in, I had gone up to bed when a neighbor called to say that there was a light on downstairs. I guess she was afraid that I might have left a candle burning. I thanked her and went down to check, only to find that the keeping room was absolutely dark. Just as I was leaving the room I felt something soft and warm brush my leg. I thought it was my dog, and clicked on a lamp. The dog wasn't in the room. When I went back upstairs I found him happily curled up on the foot of my bed.

"I had never formed much of an opinion one way or the other about ghosts, but that night I *knew* that something large and solid had brushed against me. It wasn't unpleasant, just a little odd.

"Over the years, I heard other stories about the place. Susan Sevrens, who has since passed away, once rented the house. She went home for lunch one day and walked into the keeping room, only to see, in broad daylight, a woman in full colonial dress slipping out the far door. When she followed the woman,

Mrs. Sevrens could find no one. As she had thought, she was alone in the house. Janie Wallach also lived here for a number of years. She told me that none of her cats would voluntarily go into the keeping room. If she carried them in, their hair would stand on end and they would scramble out of her arms.

"There is a story about this place. It involves Judith Chase, a rich Quaker who at one time owned the property. She apparently used to sit in the keeping room and count her silver every night. One evening, she found a spoon missing. She called the servant girl into the room and accused her of having taken it. Despite the girl's protestations of innocence, she was fired. The girl was apparently unable to find work after that and she starved to death. It is said to be her spirit that returns to the house.

"Now, here's a funny thing. Helen Backus Shaw, who I believe was born in the house, once told me that her grandfather, when cleaning the fireplace, found a single silver spoon hidden up on a ledge in the keeping-room chimney. I've often wondered about that one silver spoon."

A Woman in the Fireplace

Jack and Clair Vandenberg bought the house in the spring of 1972. It was a "depressing" house, as Mrs. Vandenberg said; it was dank and musty and smelled of rotting wood. They scrubbed, painted, restored, repaired, rewired, put in new plumbing fixtures, and brought in their own furniture. To Mrs. Vandenberg's dismay, the unhealthy smell still clung.

Located off Orange Street on the outskirts of town, the house was built around 1835. It is one and three-quarter stories, shingled, and has a stone foundation and a ridge chimney. The present chimney is original. Heat provided by an oil furnace comes up through floor grates downstairs, but there is no heat on the second floor. There are four big fireplaces, two upstairs and two down, and a gas stove in the kitchen. A large wooden storage closet is built into the wall next to the kitchen fireplace downstairs.

One day shortly after the family moved there, Mrs. Vandenberg went to the storage closet for a bucket. She was reaching toward the back of the closet, one foot inside, when she felt a shock of panic and "absolute fear" as acute as an electrical current. She snatched her hand back, leaped out, and slammed the door. She says, quite simply, that she was overcome by something that "wasn't good" and was "active or alive" in that closet. She insists that the feeling was instinctive and in no way interpretive, and Mrs. Vandenberg is not a skittish sort of woman. Her reaction was pure reflex, for the scare was too immediate to allow time for thought.

The experience was the first of many like it that happened near the fireplaces in the house. The feeling was one of being bullied by someone; there would suddenly be "something there" in the area of one of the fireplaces. Mrs.

Vandenberg noticed that the upstairs closet next to the fireplace, directly above that first-floor closet, also seemed to have its moments. The second-floor closet has a wooden door in the ceiling that opens up to an additional storage area. Several times as Mrs. Vandenberg went to get a blanket or sheets, she had a prickly sensation and a strange feeling that someone was looking down at her from behind that ceiling door.

At times, the fireplace closets felt perfectly normal, and the idea of these strange visitations appeared ridiculous. In addition, the intrusions always seemed to happen when her children and husband were not around; she began to wonder whether she was just imagining things. When Jack had a similar experience, quite out of character for him, she was both relieved and worried. According to Mrs. Vandenberg, he has neither interest nor patience where paranormal phenomena are concerned. Nevertheless, when he was alone in the house one day, he apparently felt a rush of that same intangible threat. He later told her that he suddenly knew that there was something "pushing" at him in the house. To his own surprise, he found himself yelling, "This is our house now and you get out of here!" Husband and wife felt equally silly about their dramatic reactions, but couldn't seem to help themselves. The feeling of an intruder was unpleasant and scary.

One of the oddest details of the story is Mrs. Vandenberg's experience of an idea that "would keep forming itself" in her mind, like an irritating song heard too many times on the radio. The idea was that something abusive had happened to a twenty-eight-year-old woman in the house. The woman had black hair, wore long, dark clothes, and was very angry. The image was a specific one. Mrs. Vandenberg tried to shake the idea when it ran through her mind, and was amused by the fact that the woman seemed suspiciously like a character lifted from a bad gothic novel; but she found that the thought would return with a strange persistence.

Next to the fireplace upstairs is a heavy Empire chest of drawers that the Vandenbergs brought with them. It sits against the wall, about two and a half feet from the edge of the fireplace. The drawers have metal knobs, and are graduated in size. Mrs. Vandenberg had been hearing a very faint clinking noise, like the sound of coins or keys being jingled together, coming from the direction of the bureau. The sound was just the "tiniest vibration," and would go on for several hours at a stretch. She checked the knobs on the bureau, finding them tightly screwed on, and then tried unplugging all the electrical appliances in the house to see if the clinking was being caused by a machine or lamp. It was not. The sound was coming from one of the center drawers, and yet there was nothing in the drawer itself that could be making the noise. She tried pulling the drawer out of the bureau. If she held it tightly enough, the noise would stop, only to start again as soon as she loosened her grip. This intermittent clinking went on for two months or so until one day she lost her temper. Feeling foolish, but too frazzled to care, she said firmly, "Now this is enough! I've really had enough!" The noise stopped abruptly, and she has never heard it again.

This shed new light on the problem. Whatever was in the house was apparently capable of interacting, for it seemed to respond to a firm reprimand. Mrs. Vandenberg had occasionally been aware of something near one of the fireplaces, something more defined and slightly firmer than the invisible feeling of threat. Although she never actually saw anything, she described it as being like "a displacement of air," comparing it to a small-scale version of the change in air pressure one feels when being passed by a car on the highway. It was a "using-up of space, as if the air in the room was being pushed toward me or around me." She felt that it was sometimes an object about her own size, and at other times something perhaps twice the size of a person. The feeling it gave was not like that of a breeze or a gust, but was simply a perceptible change in air density.

One night when she and her young son were upstairs, she distinctly heard a woman moaning, as if in pain from inside the fireplace. Although instinctively horrified, she did everything she could to misinterpret the sound. She was reading in bed at the time, and got up and checked on her son, who was asleep in his room. That, however, was merely a gesture, for she knew that the low wailing was not one a child could make. She stuck her head out the window in the hope that the sound was coming from outside. It was not. She was sure that it wasn't the wind or an animal; it was unmistakably human.

She had found that when she thought *at* whatever it was, in a kind but firm way ("Now, we're not going to start that again," or, "Just stop this, right now,") the intruding presence would fade. She concentrated, and tried this with the moaning. It stopped. Aside from the intermittent clinking in the bureau, this was the only time she had heard a sound connected with the disturbance.

Gradually, the threatening presence seemed to be leaving the house, for it made itself felt less frequently, and became fainter in its manifestations. Mrs. Vandenberg observed that its disappearance involved a battle of wills. If she became even slightly panicky or tried to ignore it, it "grew stronger." She hasn't felt it for four or five years now. The dank, unhealthy smell that formerly permeated the house also faded, and finally disappeared for good. Mrs. Vandenberg says she doesn't care what the source of these disturbances was, nor does she think about it much anymore; she is just thankful that it has finally gone.

George Cushman

"I rented a small house on Prospect Street in the summer of 1945. The war was over, and I was there alone with my two-year-old daughter, Betsy, waiting for my husband to come back from overseas. The island was filled with young war wives at the time. Many of the houses were boarded up. We all rode bikes to and from the store, and it was unusually peaceful and quiet. The island still had the subdued feeling that it had had during the worst of the war years.

"The house is a pre-Revolutionary saltbox with two front rooms, which were once used as parlors, and a larger keeping room behind. I had set up my bed and Betsy's cot in the left parlor. At night, the street lamps illuminated the room. The house had a friendly feeling to it. Although I was only twenty-four, I never felt lonely or uncomfortable there.

"This particular experience was an isolated incident. I had spent the evening in the keeping room with a friend. We had been talking about this and that, and making argyle socks in front of the fire. My friend left at about ten o'clock and I went to bed and fell asleep immediately.

"I was awakened in the night by the *thump-click* sound of a latch being lifted. I turned over and saw a short, elderly man crossing the room. He had apparently just entered by the keeping-room door, for it was still swinging open behind him, and he was headed toward the other door, which opens from our bedroom into the front hall. Dressed in oilskins, he was long in the body and short in the legs. He had a swordfisherman's cap on, and was carrying a pail. He never gave any sign that he was aware of my presence, and was halfway across the bedroom, walking at a normal pace, when I said something like 'What are you doing in here?' As I spoke, he vanished.

"I knew it was only a nightmare, but I was badly shaken. I got Betsy and put her in bed with me. Curling up with the baby, I closed my eyes and eventually went back to sleep.

"In the morning I noticed that the bedroom door, which I always closed at night, was open. It's impossible for one of those deep latch fittings to open by itself. The goose flesh rose on my neck. I gathered Betsy up and went over to my neighbor's house. A sensible, brusque word or two was what I needed. Mrs. Olney Dunham was a straightforward Scandinavian woman who called a spade a spade. I told her what had happened to me, and described the little man in detail. She looked at me oddly and said, 'Why, George Cushman's been dead for years!' "

William Coffin's House

The house was built in 1808. It stood at the head of Main Street, presiding over the town until 1817, when it was moved to its present location on Union Street to make way for the new Pacific National Bank building. The house belonged to William Coffin.

Mr. Coffin was a victim in the notorious 1795 robbery of the Nantucket Bank. Located on the south side of Main Street near Union, the bank was the first to be established on the island and only the third in Massachusetts. It was organized by a group of people with political and financial influence in the community. Some friction was to be expected, for the stakes were high and the founders had varying opinions on how such a business should be run. No one, however, expected a conflict such as the one that soon followed.

Less than two weeks after the bank opened, $21,000 disappeared from the vault overnight. The directors and stockholders of the bank turned against each other, and the town was wracked with backbiting and gossip. The theft seemed too clean not to have been done by someone thoroughly familiar with the bank, but there was no conclusive evidence as to who had done it. Years of litigation and irreversible personal damage were followed by the confession, twenty-one years after the robbery, of a convict in a New York State prison. He was one of three professional burglars who had arrived in Nantucket harbor on a sloop, done the job, and left unnoticed at daybreak. No Nantucketer had touched the money.

William Coffin was a director of the bank, and one of those most active in promoting its establishment. He was a respected, though controversial, figure in the community. Many of the deals that originated in his wig shop in town caused tongue-clickings and general disapproval, but Coffin was a shrewd investor who had shown himself capable of making money, and was fast becoming a local political force to be reckoned with. He was in his thirties when he became involved with the bank, and had already been postmaster as well as wig-maker. Intelligent, ambitious, Machiavellian by nature, he was more successful than popular.

Whatever his reputation had been prior to the robbery, it was certainly not improved by his indictment before the Suffolk County Supreme Court in 1797. Families had been pulled apart by anger and suspicion over the theft, and William Coffin was later to sue and actually beat up his distant cousin, Micajah Coffin. A local religious pamphlet published in 1807 declared that the inhabitants of Nantucket ". . . no longer live together like a family of brothers . . . They hate and revile and persecute each other . . . It is hoped that when the present generation, with their prejudices and rancour shall have passed off the stage, the generation which succeeds will be restored to the sincerity, the good faith, the unsuspecting candour and the brotherly affection of former times . . ." In his own pamphlet, written shortly after the robbery, William Coffin claimed that he had been victimized by "chicanery," "phrenzy," and "moon-struck madness." He died a bitter man.

Coffin's house is a two-and-a-half-story, Federal-style building. The iron railing on the front is the one that was on the steps of the Nantucket Bank when it was robbed in 1795. The house is formal and prepossessing; one can easily imagine it standing at the head of Main Street.

Peter Benchley, best identified as author of the book *Jaws*, spent a summer alone in the house in the late 1960s. At the time, it was owned by Marjorie Mills. The author had a strange experience that he says is clear to this day. He was in the house alone, and woke up from an afternoon nap in one of the bedrooms to see a fire burning in the fireplace and an old man sitting in front of the fire in a rocking chair, rocking gently. He had long hair and was dressed in eighteenth-century clothing. By the time Peter was fully awake, the man had vanished. There was no fire, and the chair was still. Benchley is convinced that what he saw was not a dream.

Marjorie Mills, who had loaned him the house as a summer workplace, was not surprised by his experience. She said that she had reason to believe the house had ghosts, but the details of her story have been lost, and she is no longer alive to recount the tale.

In 1970, Mr. and Mrs. John Tanner bought the house. Mrs. Tanner, who has since passed away, said in 1979 that it had been a peaceful house with the exception of a few inexplicable happenings.

In early spring, just after they had moved in, Mrs. Tanner was cleaning in the kitchen when she heard a crash from the library next door. She ran into the room and found that all the books from the middle shelf of a small standing bookcase were on the floor. The bookcase, enclosed on three sides, has sturdy wooden shelves that lift out of adjustable metal brackets. She knelt down and examined the middle shelf, which was still securely in place. The case would have to have been tipped forward in order for those books to fall, which would have emptied at least the top shelf too. Alternatively, someone would have had to reach in with a strong arm to sweep all the books off the middle shelf. A friend later suggested that she should have looked at the books themselves for an answer to their odd behavior, but a surprised Mrs. Tanner simply reshelved them and went back to the kitchen. She doesn't remember what the specific titles were, for they were in the house when the Tanners bought it and have since been sold.

Several years later, Mrs. Tanner woke up at 4:00 A.M. to a loud whirring noise. She said it sounded exactly like a city streetcleaner's truck. She put on her bathrobe and went downstairs, only to find the empty electric blender in the kitchen buzzing away at high speed. The machine was a new and expensive one that had been used only two or three times. Mrs. Tanner was fascinated, for the appropriate push-button controls were indeed down. She wondered if a short-circuit or electrical surge could have turned it on and pulled in the buttons. That, however, seemed doubtful, and the Tanners began to joke about a resident ghost.

A third occurrence was even more puzzling. The guest bedroom upstairs had twin four-poster beds with detachable urn-shaped knobs on the tops. The knobs were hand-turned and distinctive in shape. Mrs. Tanner was cleaning the attic one day, and came across a familiar-looking knob tucked away in a box of buttons, screws, and household extras. She brought it downstairs, and to her amazement found that it was one of the eight knobs to the beds. She had no idea how long the knob to the bedpost had been missing, for the guest room had been closed up for several months.

The Tanners' ghost experiences might be passed off as having some natural explanation. Many residents in town, however, will mention the house on Union Street when asked about Nantucket ghosts. It seems that generations of owners have murmured, *sotto voce*, to neighbors and friends about goings-on in the house. The building has a reputation for being slightly out of the ordinary. But then, its original owner was no ordinary man.

Mermaid

"I'll tell you about something that happened to me about three years ago in the Whaling Museum. I don't want you to use my name. I'm sure I'd think it was laughable if it hadn't been me.

"My sister was on-island for a visit. It was a warmish spring day, and I suggested that we walk over to the Whaling Museum. We had both been there dozens of times before, but belonging as we do to an old Nantucket family, we have always been interested in the island's history. Well, we looked at the whaling gear and the big whale skeleton, and went through most of the museum. As we were just about ready to go, I was standing alone in a room of portraits, just looking around. My sister was out in the hall. Suddenly, I was aware of being stared at. Turning around, I looked right at the portrait of a pleasant-faced young man. He had regular features, nothing you might call distinctive. Now this sounds weird, but I was absolutely sure that I knew him—not recognized him, but *knew* him. The sensation was crystal clear. I hadn't the tiniest doubt that he and I were intimate friends, and had been for a long time, and the feeling was so overwhelming that I could only keep thinking, 'I *know* you! I *know* you!' It was as if he were my long-lost husband, but also as if it were happening to someone other than me. I'm a happily married woman, and this kind of thing is hardly in character. I was transfixed, absolutely absorbed, and that was part of what was so scary. I was held by a magnetism of some kind that was so strong I couldn't move. It wasn't that I was objectively interested in him, or thought I saw a family resemblance of some kind. It was rather that he had an iron grip on me.

"The next thing I knew, my sister had me by the arm and was pulling me out of the room, shaking me and asking what was wrong. She'd been standing in the doorway calling my name, and then watching me stare as if in a trance at this portrait. Even when we were out in the sunlight, I just wanted to get back and see that man, and kind of be with him. In all my previous visits to the museum, I don't remember ever having glanced twice at that portrait before.

"My sister was so unnerved by the way I had acted that I became scared, too, and went to my minister. He told me a story that really did me in. Now, before we get into what he told me, let me mention one thing. Ever since I was a child, I've had a recurrent 'memory,' I guess you'd call it, that pops into my mind from time to time. It's not a dream; it drifts across my thoughts when I'm fully awake. I've wondered from the time I was little where it came from and what it meant. It goes like this: I remember being in pitch blackness and having an excruciating pain in my side as I swim back and forth, back and forth, in black water. I also remember phosphorescence around me, the kind you see in the ocean on a dark night. I always thought it was peculiar, and I used to tell myself that maybe it was a memory of being inside the womb or something. I had told my husband about it, but no one else.

"When I went to see my minister after that experience in the museum, he said, trying to make me smile, 'Oh, my goodness! Don't you know the legend about that picture?' I said no, I didn't. He explained that the man in the painting had supposedly been in love with a mermaid, and that his wife was very jealous. She had a special silver-tipped harpoon made to kill this mermaid, and apparently hired someone who succeeded in carrying out the deed. Well, that, of course, made me think of that swimming memory I have. The whole thing just seemed too horribly coincidental, although I don't, of course, believe in mermaids.

"I haven't been back in the Whaling Museum since that day, although for months afterward I had a terrible craving to go back and see that painting. I'm a grown woman with grandchildren, but I would wake up in the middle of the night all upset, seeing that man's face as clear as day in my mind, and my husband would have to comfort me. I had trouble eating and sleeping. I was praying, all that time, that the man in that painting wouldn't bother me anymore. The feeling of being magnetically drawn to that portrait to the point of obsession finally faded, thank God, but I'll never go back to the Whaling Museum as long as I live. I'm not that curious."

A Very Large Chin

Jesse is seven years old. Her father and stepmother were invited to a party on India Street one July evening in 1981. Jesse came along with a bag of stuffed animals, crayons, and paper to keep herself amused.

She had exhausted her supplies by the time dinner was served. It was 9:00, and she was understandably cranky and tired. One of the guests suggested that she take an inventory of the first floor, noting down on her pad all the mirrors, all the candlesticks, all the brass doorknobs, and so forth. She thought that sounded interesting. The dinner guests could soon hear her busily counting away in the adjoining rooms and hallways.

A rambling, Federal-style structure, the house was built in 1831 by James Childs, the master carpenter who, with Christopher Capen, built the Three Bricks on Main Street. In 1972, the house was given to its present owners, Anne and Patrick Perkins, by an elderly woman named Emily Hunt. Mrs. Hunt's husband had died several years before she met the Perkinses.

Jesse had been quietly working on her project for a good half-hour when she came running into the dining room, shrieking that she had seen a man in the library. She was shaking, pale, and genuinely frightened. She blurted out that she had walked into the room and seen a man with a very large chin and a strange, dark-blue suit standing near a pair of rubber beach sandals that someone had left on the rug. He had tipped his hat to her, taken a couple of steps away from her, and vanished. She didn't mention the word ghost, and when questioned by her skeptical parents, simply reiterated how long his chin was. She said that he had looked at her with a "friendly, unscary face," and that he hadn't said anything.

None of the adults present took her experience too seriously, and she soon seemed to forget about it herself, settling down at her seat to have dessert with the grown-ups. In the weeks that followed, she didn't mention the experience to her parents again. The Perkinses had never seen or heard of a ghost in their house, and had also more or less forgotten Jesse's unlikely story until the following incident took place about a month later.

Jesse and her parents were visiting late one afternoon, and one of Mrs. Perkins's daughters brought out a line drawing that looked as though it had been done from a group photograph of a garden party. Clothing and people's hairstyles placed the date of the drawing between 1940 and 1950. It had been found in the attic that day in the course of a search through old boxes for a missing item. The print was passed around as a curiosity, and Jesse, who was on the floor drawing a picture, took a casual look at it. Her face lit right up, and she said excitedly, "There he is! That's him! There he is!" She pointed to a middle-aged man sitting with a woman underneath a shade umbrella. He did indeed have an extraordinarily prominent, square chin. He was identified, from a key on the back of the drawing, as Emily Hunt's husband, William. The Perkinses did some research on the man, hoping to find out more about him, but only came up with his death date, 1961, and the fact that he had committed suicide.

A Little Girl

"My son Jimmy suffered the most from this whole experience. He was just old enough to be really traumatized by what he had seen. He would never stay alone in the house after that, even during the day, and he would get jumpy and irritable when asked about her."

Joanne and Jim Shaw and their two children moved to the island from Rochester, New York, in 1972. Jim gave up his insurance business, and has worked since '72 as a fisherman. Joanne teaches dance classes and works at Even Keel, a clothing store on Main Street. The Shaws rented one of the old farmhouses in Polpis, on the north side of the island, from 1976 to 1980.

Joanne went on: "Jimmy was nine at the time. He and his sister Erin, who was six, had adjoining bedrooms upstairs; Jim and I slept on the first floor. Jimmy woke up one night to see a little girl standing in the dark by the side of his bed. He said, half asleep, 'What do you want, Erin?' When she didn't move or answer, it began to dawn on him that something was wrong. He jumped out of the other side of the bed and ran into Erin's room. She was fast asleep. He woke up his sister, and the two of them came thumping and shrieking downstairs and dove into bed with us. Jimmy was terrified, and had trouble sleeping for weeks afterward. In fact, we could never get him and Erin to sleep upstairs again. We eventually stopped trying, and set up a little bedroom for them down near ours.

"My husband and I thought Jimmy had probably had a bad nightmare, and we didn't pay much attention to his story. I did realize, however, that he was genuinely terrified by the memory of that little child.

"About a week later, all four of us were jammed into the double bed (Jim and I still hoping the kids would get over this and go back upstairs). It was a sticky, hot August night. All I could hear was the constant, piercing whine of mosquitoes. Each time one of us slapped, the others would get bounced, bumped, or woken up. I was in the middle. Finally I got up and stretched out on the living room couch. I was lying on my back, just drifting off, when I saw a little girl standing in the shadows on the other side of the room. She looked slightly taller than Erin. As I opened my eyes completely, she began to walk toward me. I remember that she was wearing a dark kerchief tied under her chin. Although I couldn't make out her facial features or the details of her body, I was aware that she was walking slowly, not drifting or floating. She had a long skirt or dress on. My first reaction to her approach was a strange one, and perhaps instinctive; I felt that she had mistaken me for her mother, and that she was coming over as if to give me a hug or nestle up to me. I felt a sudden rush of panic as she reached the end of the couch. I leaped up, exclaiming 'What in heck—!' As soon as I spoke, she vanished.

"I had never seen an apparition before, and would never have counted myself among the believers of such things; however, this child was real. She was no dream. The sight of her approaching me, her head hidden in that little kerchief, is still as vivid as can be—and it still gives me goose bumps.

"I was objectively curious about this little person; but I was also shaken. The idea that she might have mistaken me for her own mother was pathetic but, more than that, alarming; after all, my family and I had to go on living in the house. I guess I also felt vaguely guilty that I had jumped up from the couch. I had an unpleasant, lingering certainty that she had wanted something from me. I still wonder, at odd moments, what might have happened if I hadn't moved.

"I brought the kids' things downstairs the next day and we converted a small room off the front hallway into a bedroom for them. I told my husband about having seen Emily, as we later named her, on the night it happened. I told my kids the next morning, and Jimmy was reassured to hear that I had also seen the little girl. I tried to present the experience in a matter-of-fact way. If we had to share the house with a ghost, I thought it was best that we try to be straightforward about it.

"I did look into the history of the house. It was built in the first quarter of the nineteenth century. I talked with some of the older Nantucketers in Polpis, but they didn't remember hearing of any strange incidents connected with the property. The little girl, of course, could conceivably have died many generations ago.

"A couple of weeks later, on a stormy, windy night, Emily turned up again. Jim had set the alarm for 3 A.M. in order to go out fishing. Shortly before the alarm went off, we were awakened from a sound sleep by a howling just outside our bedroom window. It really didn't sound like a domestic dog; the tone was closer to that of a coyote. It was probably someone's stray, caught in the storm, but it sure was a desolate, eerie sound. Neither one of us could get back to sleep, and Jim got up to take his shower.

"He didn't tell me this at the time, not wanting to frighten me, but as soon as he opened our bedroom door, he could feel that there was someone out in the hallway between our room and the bathroom. I did notice that he stood in our open bedroom door for a minute or so before going down the hall. Faced with this sense of an unknown presence standing in front of him in the dark, he actually put his head down, stretched one arm out in front of him, and walked (or, rather, dove) down the dark hallway to the bathroom. He switched the light on, and looked back to find that the hall was empty. He took his shower and left the house.

"I was just dozing off again when I felt the bed go down on one side. Apparently, someone had sat down next to me. I was lying on my stomach, my arms tucked under me. I thought at first that it was one of the kids, but when no one spoke, my heart started beating faster. Before I could lift my head or look around, I felt someone sitting on my upper back—someone about the weight of a young child. I then felt—oh, God, this gives me the creeps!—a hand stroking the back of my head. I don't know whether it was five minutes or a few seconds, but it seemed to go on forever.

"I couldn't move. I don't know if you've ever had dreams where you're being pursued by something and your legs melt beneath you, but it was just that kind of feeling. I didn't seem to have any muscles. Pinned under this unseen weight, I just lay there feeling the soft, intermittent stroking on the back of my head. Then the adrenaline began to flow, and gathering all my strength, I flung myself out of bed, half falling on the floor. I remember shrieking, 'Get out of here! Get out of here!'

"Needless to say, I was up the rest of the morning. When Jim got in later in the day, and I told him, shakily, what had happened, he said, 'Oh, yes, she was out in the hallway when I got up.' I could have killed him for not telling me before he left the house!

"There were times when I would walk into my bedroom during the day and feel that she was sitting on a caned chair in the corner by one of the windows. I couldn't see anything, but I would look over there and then I would hear a rustle from the chair seat, as if someone had just stood up. This would be followed by sequential creaking of the floorboards, as if she were walking around the edge of the room. The creaking always followed the same route, moving around by the wall, in front of my dresser, and out the door. It was as if I had disturbed her, and she got up and left the room.

"The following winter we went to Florida for a couple of weeks. I packed everything away and closed up the house. When we got home, I opened the front door to find hundreds of dead blackflies in the foyer. They were great big horseflies, the kind you don't usually see inside in the winter. They were so thick underfoot that I swept up a big dustpan-full of them. What a horrible welcome! Even worse, when I went to put the kids to bed, I turned back their covers and found that both of their beds were filled with the same kind of large dead flies. They were under the covers, as if someone had turned back each bed, thrown the flies in on the bottom sheet, and then made the beds up.

"Although Jimmy only saw Emily that one night, he definitely had a harder time dealing with her apparent existence than the rest of us did. As long as we lived in that house, he was afraid of being alone, couldn't sleep, and worried that he would see her again. I must admit that my initial feeling of sympathy for the little girl changed pretty rapidly to one of apprehension and, after that experience in the bedroom, simple horror. The sight of her, the feeling of being pinned on my bed and having someone touching the back of my head, the creaking sounds, the blackflies—living with that unknown child is something I'll never forget."

Sixteen Men

"Grace and I were alone in the house, sleeping in adjoining bedrooms. We had spent the evening at home, had two glasses of wine apiece with dinner, and had taken nothing alcoholic since then. Grace got up at 2:15 A.M. for an extra blanket, and happened to look out the window. There were several people outside. She came into my room and woke me up."

This incident occurred in 1977, on the Friday before Halloween. Marcia Hart, who now lives on Nantucket, was then a student at Brown University. She had come to the island for the weekend to visit her friend Grace Patterson; it was Grace's first winter on Nantucket, and she was renting a new house on the outskirts of town. The two young women had become friends during a summer of waitressing together. Marcia continued:

"We left the lights out, and stood by the window in Grace's bedroom. It was below freezing, and there was plenty of starlight but no moon. The backyard had no grass or trees, for it had only recently been cleared. It consisted of about fifty square yards of mounded dirt and sand, which ended at the back of the Chicken Box bar. On the left was an unpaved parking lot, and on the right a new house. Sure enough, about ten feet from the back of the bar, I could see six men in white pants. Their shirts were dark, and there was not enough light to see their features clearly. They didn't appear to be wearing bulky winter clothing. They were lifting and tugging a large, heavy object about the size and shape of a shipping crate, or of a refrigerator laid on its side. Occasionally one or another of them would straighten up and stop for rest. There was no wind, and while we could hear low voices, we couldn't make out any words. Now and then we could hear the scrabble of loose pebbles as a boot scraped on the frozen ground.

"I called the police. Soon we could hear the patrol car coming, and as the headlights swept across the yard, the men got down on all fours and rolled into the deep, irregular troughs between the heaps of dirt. Two patrolmen climbed out and, standing next to their car, beamed their flashlights back and forth. Nothing to be seen. The rear of the building was thrown into shadow by the headlights, and the large object the men had been trying to move was not visible. It was a bitterly cold night, so without having left the side of their car, after a quick look around, the patrolmen climbed back in and drove away.

"We saw the men crawl up out of the ditches as the taillights disappeared down the street. They went on with their work as more of them appeared from the front side of the building; soon a dozen men were taking turns at moving the large rectangular object.

"Four men were hoisted up onto the roof of the building. We could see first one and then another crouching in silhouette on the ridge, apparently talking to the men below. A figure was sitting in the driver's seat of my VW bug, which I had left unlocked. He was bobbing up and down as if he were working on something down near the floor. Feet crossed and recrossed the line of light under the back door of the bar; it seemed that the men had gotten inside the building.

"Several hours went by as we pointed out different figures to each other and tried to keep track of how many there were. The men moved lightly, with rapid, animated motions, and none of them looked very tall. We were tense, and careful not to let them see us. I remember feeling strangely lucid. Looking back, I'm puzzled and surprised—and troubled—that we didn't immediately call the police again. After all, we were sitting by, glued to the window, whispering to each other while we watched a bunch of men robbing a bar. That's not exactly a normal reaction, and not the kind of thing either of us would do. It makes me wonder if those men had some sort of numbing effect on us. I suppose we were waiting until the sky lightened and we could see what the men were doing, although that now seems like an inadequate explanation.

"Shortly after 4:30, we counted sixteen men behind the Chicken Box. The large object had been moved approximately twenty feet along the back of the building. The figures seemed to be taking turns at different activities: some climbed up on the roof, others moved this object, still others just walked back and forth. We watched until dawn. As the sky began to lighten, it became apparent to us both that the figures were fading. They continued with their activities, but were becoming increasingly difficult to see. We were appalled. I felt suddenly nauseous, and Grace just kept saying, 'Oh, my God! This is ridiculous!' over and over. By the time the first real flush of pink hit the sky, the yard was empty."

Neither Marcia nor Grace had ever seen an apparition or ghost before that night, nor have they since. Marcia's car battery was dead the following morning, but that was the only possible physical trace that the men had left behind. The rectangular object they had been struggling with had disappeared with them. Nathaniel Benchley, on hearing this story, remarked that the area was reputed to have been a connection point for rumrunners during Prohibition. The Chicken Box, a one-story frame building, was built in the 1950s, and is now a popular bar that stays open all year.

" Dr E P Fleming "   69. 0
    Express for Collecting Money in New Bedford   2. 0
Cash p^d Seth Cathcart & David Cathcart heirs   75
    $5 each, bequeathed to them in the Will
To Nancy M Coffin to Furniture in Front Chamber   10. 00
    & basement as per Appraisal —
To Six large Silver Spoons, & Eighteen Small do   62. 00
one Rocking Chair do   18. 00
Cash p^d Chas H Robinson for Grave Stone & Setting   3. 00
My Commissions for Services rendered   26. 50
Balance in hands of Executor —   25. 00
                                                      ‾‾‾‾‾‾
                                                       28 53
                                                      $ 289. 00

                    Cr
Household furniture as per Appraisal rendered
    to the Probate Court —
Cash from Newburyport Savings Bank, & Interest   83. 00
                                                       206. 00
                                                      $ 289. 00
            Charles Rawson Executor,
     June 3^d 1862

A Shaker Rocker

"My wife and I are antiques dealers, and bought our house on Union Street in September of 1967. We're from Connecticut, and had opened a small branch of our mainland business on one of the wharves here the previous summer. We fell in love with the island, and began looking for a place to live at the end of the season. Once we set foot in the house, we knew immediately that it had to be ours. It all happened very quickly. We moved in, and began stripping off all kinds of trim and overlay. The floors were covered with linoleum, the fireplaces were blocked up, the lights, or small fire windows over the doors, were painted over. We unmasked the house, room by room, doing most of the restoration work ourselves.

"I looked into the history of the house and found that it had been built by Captain Joseph West in 1802. When his wife, Mary, died in 1816, West sold the house to Captain Obed Cathcart for $1,300. Cathcart lived in the house with his wife, Sally McCleave, until his death in 1861. They had no children, and the house then passed to Cathcart's niece, Nancy M. Coffin, who in turn willed it to her husband, Alfred M. Coffin. Alfred Coffin sold it to the Home for Aged People in Winchester in 1895, and Mary J. Gifford Smith bought it from them in the same year. It was sold in 1917 to Mr. and Mrs. William Hall, who owned the house until 1954, when they sold it to Arthur and Jessie Stetson. We bought it from the Stetsons, making a total of only seven families in the house over the past 181 years.

"One January day in 1968 we were working on the large fireplace in the keeping room. There was a loose board bulging out above the fireplace, and I couldn't make it lay flat. This section had been plastered over and wallpapered.

I tapped it, and it sounded hollow. We scraped and peeled and eventually pried up the board. Inside was a small cupboard with shallow shelves, the type of storage area known as a parson's cupboard. It had been sealed, from the looks of the wall, for at least a century. A small section of the shelving had dried out and disintegrated, and as we dug deeper we found several small utilitarian objects that had fallen down between the shelving and the wall: an ivory comb, a bottle, a pincushion, and a flint, all dating back to the first half of the nineteenth century. They were personal, everyday things that had probably gotten pushed into the corner of the cupboard and then fallen through the rotted area in the shelving. We put all of these little objects on the top of a sea chest sitting in the room, and left them out that night when we went to bed.

"It was a clear, moonlit winter night. My wife, Kay, and I were sleeping on a mattress in the bedroom on one side of the keeping room, and our one-year-old son was sleeping in the room on the other side. My wife woke me up at about one o'clock and asked if I would go check on our son, who was fussing a bit. I got up and started through the door of the keeping room. We had no curtains, and the room was bright in the moonlight, filled with that lovely gray-blue tone that comes from a full moon in a clear sky.

"Suddenly, I froze. A little Shaker rocking chair sitting a few feet from the fireplace was moving as if someone had just been rocking and then had stood up. You know, one—two—three, each rock smaller than the last one. As I peered into the room, trying to see if anyone was there, I had the definite feeling that I had startled someone rocking in the chair, and that the person had jumped up and hurried to the far corner of the room where a closet door stood open in the shadows. I stood still for, I guess, a couple of minutes, looking into the corner to see if I could make out anything resembling a figure. I couldn't, but I just knew there was a person, or perhaps I should say, a presence, hiding from me in the dark. I was shaken, and since our son had quieted down, I went back to bed and told Kay what had happened.

"She got up and went to the doorway. The chair had stopped moving, but to my surprise she, too, had a clear impression that someone was standing in the corner of the room. It wasn't threatening or evil, but it was a little scary. We didn't walk over to the corner or shine a light into the room out of some feeling, I suppose, that we had already disturbed that presence, whatever it was, and that we should leave well enough alone. I couldn't help wondering if our discovery of the objects in the parson's cupboard had anything to do with this weird experience.

"As we worked on the house, we began to come across the name "Obed Cathcart" in all sorts of odd places. Late one afternoon I was busy with something downstairs and felt a sudden urge to go up to the attic, which was empty at the time. I got a flashlight, went up, and found myself crawling into a little cranny in the eaves. Nailed to the wall were several pieces of what looked like an old hatbox, deep in a corner where there would ordinarily be no reason even to look. I pulled them off the wall, and on the cover of the hatbox was written in bold lettering, CAPTAIN OBED CATHCART.

"This business of feeling impelled to look in a certain place and then finding his name happened a number of times. It was as if I were suddenly directed by a firm, friendly hand toward a specific spot. I remember working one day in my son's room, where we had taken up the linoleum. I noticed a seam in the floor, and found myself digging down under the board. I popped it up, and sure enough, written on a long strip of paper were the words CAPTAIN OBED CATHCART. He had buried his name all over the house; it was as if I were satisfying some old urge of his by uncovering it.

"I did some research on the man and found that he had made several whaling voyages to the Pacific between 1826 and 1838 on the *Elizabeth Starbuck* and the *James Loper* out of Nantucket, and on the *Victory* and the *Young Phoenix* out of New Bedford. He left Nantucket again in 1850 as captain of the *Ontario*. The ship was condemned at Tahiti, and its seven-hundred-barrel cargo of sperm oil was shipped to England.

"Obed bought the house when he was twenty-eight, three years after he and his wife, Sally, were married. He lived there for the remaining forty-four years of his life, and died a poor man. He left five dollars apiece to his brothers, Seth and David. To his niece, Nancy Coffin, he willed the house; in the Probate Court inventory, he left her the furniture 'in Front chamber and basement,' appraised at $62.00; six large silver spoons and eighteen small ones, worth $18.00; and one rocking chair, worth $3.00.

"It seems strange that a whaling captain who had made so many trips should die with so little to his name. And he was apparently a good man. I have a clipping about a rescue he made from the *James Loper* in 1839. A Japanese junk, the *Chôja Maru*, was wrecked in January of that year and had been drifting for six months when it was sighted by Cathcart. He took the seven surviving crew members to Hawaii, where a certain Dr. Baldwin wrote, 'It is due to the kindness and generosity of Captain C., generosity often met with among seafaring men, . . . that not only were these sufferers provided with food and necessary clothing but . . . were landed here, with all the moveable property they had saved, including a considerable amount of money . . . all which, on their escaping the wreck, was put into the care of Capt. C., but none was reserved by way of compensation.' I have a feeling that he was a modest man, and probably a Quaker, who just never made it big.

"My wife and I came to accept, early on, the presence of a benevolent personality in the house. It's a wonderful house, and we've never been uncomfortable in it, but we definitely were sharing it in those early years. And there were times when Kay or I would see someone just flitting around the edge of a doorway, crossing a passageway, or disappearing around a corner when we knew there was no one there. We would catch a fleeting, peripheral glimpse of a back or of a piece of clothing. I remember one time when I was just starting up the stairs and saw a woman in a dress stepping quickly through the hall into the next room. I didn't think anything of it, assuming it was Kay, and went up the stairs and into the room across the way. I said something to Kay, and when I got no answer, I looked upstairs and then down only to find that she wasn't even in the house.

"That little Shaker rocker has been something of an enigma too. As a rule, my memory about where and when I acquire antiques is excellent; as you know, we're dealers, and we do a brisk business in Nantucket pieces out of our shop on North Water Street. But I can't, for the life of me, remember where that rocker came from. At some point shortly after we moved in I sold it, but I can't remember whom I sold it to, either. And I don't seem to have any sales slips on it; it's almost as though I have a mental block about that little chair. At any rate, a woman on Quince Street called me a few years ago and said she had a little Shaker rocker she wanted to get rid of. She didn't tell me why; she just said she wanted it out. I went over to pick it up, and sure enough, there was our little chair. We have it back at the house now, and ever since it has been back we've had no disturbances of any kind.

"I'll have to look that woman up and ask her why she wanted to get rid of it."

Christmas Music

Peter Guarino and Paul Willer bought 25 Orange Street in 1971. Peter recently related the following account.

"Paul and I came from Manhattan to Nantucket for a weekend in 1969, and it seemed like paradise. Although we're New Yorkers through and through, we'd had it with the city; we were both just exhausted from years of struggling with urban living, and we looked at each other and said, 'Let's do it. Let's sell it all and move to Nantucket.'

"We decided to look for a guesthouse. It took us two years of flying back and forth from the city before we found 25 Orange. The minute we set foot in it, we knew it was just right. We've named it The House of Orange.

"We had a strange but very pleasant recurring experience our first four years in the house. At midnight every Christmas Eve, we would hear organ music coming from the third floor. It lasted for about ten minutes. It wasn't any Christmas music that we recognized, but it was beautiful. When we went up there we could hear it more clearly, but we couldn't pinpoint the spot that it was coming from. Needless to say, there was no organ there.

"The third floor had been full of boxes of sheet music when we moved in. With a little research, I found out that a minister of St. Paul's Episcopal Church, a Mr. Snelling, had lived in the house for many years. He had used the third floor as his study, and apparently had an organ up there. His widow left the house to the church, and since the church was unable to use it, the house stood empty for four years before it changed hands.

"As we see it, Mr. Snelling was making up for those years when the house had no music on Christmas Eve."

The House that Killed My Father

"The house was utterly luxurious. It had every amenity one could want: marble showers, tiled floors, two ovens, lots of space, a terrific location. And yet, of all the houses Carol and I have lived in, that was the only one we really didn't like."

Bob Miller was standing, hammer in hand, in the warm April sunshine. To the left of his head swung a sign lettered ROBERT J. MILLER, HAIRDRESSERS, MEN AND WOMEN. Sounds of hammers and the buzz of a chain saw came from inside the building. Bob and his wife, Carol, were helping carpenters with preseason alterations in their store on Washington Street. Bob went on:

"Carol and I bought the house in 1976. It's on the southeast end of the island, and was started in 1964 by a man named William Cammon Bantry. He died suddenly, before the house was finished, and we bought the property from his widow. It was our first home on Nantucket, and we were all ready to love it. Our kids were excited about moving here, and we looked forward to working on the place.

"From the very first, though, the house felt funny. For instance, although it was soundly built, there were times when you were inside, sitting on a chair where no draft would seem possible, and you'd have the feeling of air moving around you, almost of unnatural breezes. We had some old English chairs with high upholstered backs and wings—chairs designed to protect one from drafts. Even sitting in those chairs, I would still feel as if something were blowing on me. We never could get the house cozy and warm in the winter.

"The fireplace in the den smoked terribly. We had a mason come to inspect the chimney more than once; he couldn't find any reason for its not drawing properly. I always blamed it on some sort of adverse air circulation in the building, but actually that didn't make much sense. We finally just gave up on fires.

"I remember that the house also had an unpleasant smell, one that seemed to come and go. It sounds funny now, but it was really quite awful. At first we thought that an animal had died under the building or in the walls. The smell resembled that of a dead dog or rotten onions. I finally went down to check the crawlspace under the house, but I didn't find anything. We discovered that the smell would come and just as suddenly go, on its own.

"The only room where we all felt comfortable was a large, enclosed back sunporch—a porch that we discovered was a later addition to the original plan of the house. We tended to gravitate toward that porch; we even put our Christmas tree out there, if you can believe it. I remember Carol saying to me that the living room was too dark for Christmas.

"The unpleasant feeling in the house affected us all, although we were reluctant at first to admit it. We're an easygoing family, but while we were living in that house little things seemed to get us irritated at each other all the time. I'm convinced, looking back on it, that something about the building itself put a strain on us all. In rational terms, there was absolutely nothing wrong: we adored Nantucket, the house itself was beautiful, the kids were doing well, our business was under way, we had no financial problems. And yet we found ourselves constantly tired and grumpy and nervous.

"It all came to a head with some unexpected visitors. I was working on the accounts, I think, when Carol and I heard some people knocking at the back door. I remember suddenly feeling that I didn't want to know who it was. I kept my head down and said to Carol, 'I don't want to see them. I really don't. I can't. I'm not going to answer it.' She gave me a strange look and went to see who it was. Normally, I enjoy people and am a pretty conversational, open type, but I didn't look up, even when I heard Carol showing these visitors around the house. When they left, she came in, looking upset, and told me that one of them was the daughter of the man who built the house. The woman had said to Carol that she and her husband had made a special trip to Nantucket just to see 'the house that killed my father.'

"I felt numb when I heard that. It sounds overly dramatic, but I really felt numb. I think those words brought to the surface an unspoken fear that there was something bad in the house, something horrible that we had been living with. And it scared me that I had acted so strangely; I hadn't, for some reason, wanted to meet Mr. Bantry's daughter. That's not like me. It's almost as if I didn't want to hear what she was going to say. That's when Carol and I began to take our feelings about the house seriously.

"Unable to forget those words, I asked around and found out that William Bantry had encountered a number of difficulties in building the house. He remarried at the time the house was under construction, and his new wife was not crazy about Nantucket. She made change after change in the plans as the building was going up. It was started in one direction, pulled down, and started in another. And then Mr. Bantry died quite unexpectedly of a heart attack.

"All of this is certainly not to say that Mr. Bantry had anything to do with the unpleasant feeling in the house. I have no idea why the place had a bad aura to it, but as soon as we sold it and moved to town in 1978, we felt a tremendous relief. Something in that house had a pernicious effect on us all."

Pepper Frazier, a real estate broker, and his wife, Libby, bought the house from the Millers. The Fraziers have two sons: Pepper, who was three years old when they moved in, and Dalton, who was three months. The Millers hadn't said anything to the Fraziers concerning their bad feelings about the house. Libby Frazier tells the following story.

"There was something very wrong with that place. From the time we first settled in, strange things kept happening to Dalton. When he was really tiny, I would sit him up on the floor, turn around to do something, and then hear the clunk of his little head on the wood. It was awful. I couldn't figure it out, for he wasn't that unsteady. It was as if someone had given him a good push. This happened many times when his brother was nowhere near him.

"There were also times over the next couple of years when he would be lying quietly in his crib and would suddenly scream out, as if he'd been pinched or startled. One morning he had a really bad scratch on his face. His father and I were beginning to feel a bit panicky.

"As you can imagine, we were reluctant to think that there could be anything in the house that was tormenting Dalton, knowing how foolish that sounded, but the poor little boy had one accident after another. Many of them happened for no plausible reason. He isn't an uncoordinated child, and it really began to appear as though someone invisible was doing things to him. He hated being alone in his bedroom. He would fall repeatedly and get all sorts of lumps, bruises, and scratches. He even hit his head so badly once that he began to hemorrhage internally. We rushed him to Massachusetts General, where they operated on him immediately. He's fine now, but looking back on it, I have to think that some force or spirit in the house took a violent dislike to the baby and was really out to hurt him.

"His father and I both saw a little figure that wasn't either one of our boys. We'd had a ghost in our house in Marblehead, so the idea of seeing one didn't scare us too much, but there was something utterly chilling about the ghost of a small child in this new house, a ghost about the same size and age as our boys. My husband saw him first. He looked outside one winter day and saw a tow-head run quickly by under the window. From what we saw of the top of his head, the child looked just like Dalton. It wasn't. The kids were nowhere near, and we had no neighbors with small children.

"I saw a little figure one day during the summer. I had been out doing errands, and just after I walked in the door a child ran by at the other end of the house. I called out, 'Hi, everybody. I'm home!' There was no answer. I looked around and realized that the boys and my husband were still at the beach. That scared me, for I was absolutely certain I had seen a little person scampering by in the house. It wasn't a peripheral flicker of something solid; it was definitely a child.

"Ever since we moved into town, Dalton has been fine. The accident-after-accident business stopped when we settled into our new house. I suppose that all of the things that happened could have had rational explanations, but I just know, perhaps intuitively, that they didn't. When I think back on how that house felt, what happened to Dalton in it, and the little child my husband and I both saw, I just know there was something very wrong."

Brushing My Cheek

"I told a few people about this experience back when it was going on, and they made fun of me. Know what I mean? Told me I was crazy. I kept quiet about it after that."

Mr. and Mrs. David Greenberg were, for many years, the proprietors of a family restaurant on Nantucket, and are well-loved citizens of the island. Their house, built in 1847, is in the center of town.

Mr. Greenberg leaned over, clicked off the evening news, and settled back in his chair.

"Let's see now. I guess it would have been 1952 or '53. I was awakened in the night several times during that two-year period by the feeling of someone brushing a hand softly across my cheek, just like this, lightly stroking the side of my face. It was pleasant, gentle. I would open my eyes and see a vague form of a woman drifting across our room near the foot of the bed. There's a word for it, can't think what, like protoplasm—something that moves and changes shape. She was filmy, know what I mean? She didn't walk; she moved smoothly. She wore a long, loose gown. She wasn't solid enough for me to make out her features or her expression. And—now, this is peculiar—she never made me nervous. I was startled, but not nervous. I knew, without thinking, that she was a kind person. Don't know why. Just sensed it. By the time I was awake enough to nudge my wife, there was nothing there."

Mrs. Greenberg put down her needlework. "I always believed my husband, although I never actually saw her. He and I didn't pay much attention to these nighttime visitations; we were busy, and we just took it in stride. We never told our children about it, not seeing any reason to scare them with it, and not knowing quite what to make of it ourselves.

"One Thanksgiving, when our daughter Mary was five or six, she told me that a strange lady had stood by her bed during the night.

" 'Oh?' I said. 'And what was she like, dear?'

" 'She was a nice lady, Mommy.' Those were her first words. She went on to tell me that the woman had a long neck, and was wearing a funny, floor-length dress with a high collar. She explained that the figure looked just like one of the Pilgrims. Mary wasn't at all scared. In fact, she was emphatic about liking this woman. The 'nice lady' stood by her bed, smiled down at her, and walked out of her bedroom and into ours. Mary watched her go and then rolled over and apparently went right back to sleep."

Mr. Greenberg picked up the story. "I saw the woman that same night. I woke to the familiar sensation of a soft stroking on the side of my face, but this time, when I opened my eyes, she was standing right by the side of the bed, looking down at me. She was much more distinct than before, almost solid, and I remember her as having a kind expression, although I couldn't see her features clearly. Her neck *was* very long, and bent strangely to the side, know what I mean? I don't know why it didn't spook me. I remember wondering, at the time, if her neck were bent that way because she had been hanged. Maybe she was slightly deformed. Who knows? After a few moments, she turned away and walked through the closed door of our closet and disappeared.

"We never saw her again."

Expecting the Inexplicable

The house is a multilayered structure. Over the past century and a half, the original building has been added on to many times. It is hard to tell what came after what, for some of the additions were once freestanding houses. While the clapboard exterior has an organized appearance, the interior structure is confusing in a pleasant way: floor planking changes direction and tone, ceilings rise and sink, baseboards meet up with each other with the awkward amiability of distant cousins.

Mr. and Mrs. Allan Shriver bought the house in 1966. When interviewed in 1980, they described the variety of things that happened there as "fantastic." During their first summer in the house, the family returned from the beach late one July afternoon. Walking with bare feet across the dining room to the kitchen, Mrs. Shriver stepped on a small wet spot on the rug. She doubled back to take a look. The ceiling wasn't leaking, and nothing had been spilled or overturned. Oddly enough, the pad underneath the rug was bone-dry. It didn't seem possible.

The spot got bigger and bigger over the next few days, spreading imperceptibly from the size of a dinner plate to a circle over three feet in diameter. Sopping didn't help. Mrs. Shriver called the plumber. He came to the house but was also unable to figure out where the spot came from. This went on for about a month. They simply tromped around or across the huge wet spot, for there wasn't much they could do. One morning it disappeared as suddenly as it had come, leaving no odor, residue, or stain.

Two months later, in September, the Shrivers' son Christopher came for a visit. Christopher went out with some friends one evening, and his parents had a dinner engagement. Mrs. Shriver had made a point of asking Christopher not to bring friends back to the house late that night.

The Shrivers left the dinner party and went to bed early. Mrs. Shriver wasn't feeling well, and hadn't had anything to drink for at least forty-eight hours. (She emphasizes this detail, knowing that skeptics love to connect ghosts with dinner wine.) Lying in bed, she heard the clock strike twelve, followed by the sounds of Christopher and his friends coming in. Subdued giggling, talking, and the clinking of ice in glasses drifted up the stairs. She was irritated, but decided to wait until the following morning to speak to him about it. She heard the group babbling away for a good hour; then the clock struck one. When Christopher tiptoed up the stairs at about quarter past one, she called him into her room. She whispered a fierce "Now look, dear—" from the bed, and he simply stood in the doorway, shrugged, turned on his heel, and marched down the hall to his room. He slammed the door.

Over breakfast the next morning she asked him why he had been so inconsiderate. Christopher was surprised. He told her that he hadn't come home until 3:30, and had been alone and gone right to bed. There was, indeed, no evidence of a late party downstairs. She found it hard to believe. She knew what she had heard, and he knew what he had done; they argued back and forth. The incident was so odd that Christopher brought his friends over to vouch for him. He was evidently telling the truth, for he had been at a neighbor's house until after 3:00 A.M. In thinking over the experience, Mrs. Shriver remembered that in the darkness she had seen the outline of his figure standing in the doorway, but had been unable to see his face. As crazy as it seemed, the sounds she heard and the figure she saw evidently had nothing to do with Christopher. It was at this point that the family began to joke, incredulously, about a resident ghost.

Several weeks after this happened, the Shrivers were sitting downstairs alone when they heard someone pacing back and forth in their bedroom. An even, deliberate step traversed the length of the room, paused, and walked back. It sounded like the firm, leather-soled step of a man, and went on for a good ten or fifteen minutes. The pacing occurred frequently over the next three years, and the Shrivers soon paid no more attention to it than they might have to a ticking clock or a squeaking door. It was never heard when anyone was upstairs, nor did it happen at any special time of day or in any particular weather.

At times, when they were in their bedroom, they heard a sharp, staccato rapping on the door. Mr. Shriver described it as an imperative "Goddammit, I want to talk to you" type of knocking, loud enough to awaken both of them from a sound sleep. Unlike the pacing, which had the self-absorbed rhythm of someone brooding, the rapping was angry and urgent. When he got out of bed and opened the door, there was never anyone there.

In 1966 and '67, when they were frequently hearing the footsteps and the rapping, the Shrivers lived alone in the house. Around this time they also had a problem with slamming doors, which would clap shut with a ferocious bang on still nights when no draft could be detected.

Most of these abnormal goings-on stopped after several years. Whatever was in the house seemed to quiet down. Then, one May, they had what must be one of the most generous and imaginative poltergeist visitations on record.

The Shrivers have a miniature nineteenth-century desk in their living room. About two feet high, it was probably a furniture-maker's showroom model. When Mrs. Shriver bought it, back in the late 1950s in New York, one of its five drawers was missing an ivory pull. The knobs are the size of almonds and have a distinctive yellow patina that can only come from age and wear. Each knob is ringed with tiny carved bands. The Shrivers didn't attempt to replace the missing pull.

When opening up the house recently, the Shrivers found the French doors dividing the living room from the porch stuck closed. The doors are about fifteen feet from the desk, and fasten with a vertical lock that slides into a small square hole in the floor. When they finally shot the rod up, they found an ivory pull jammed into the lock bed. The pull is indistinguishable from the other four on the desk, and is similarly worn with age. Surprisingly, it wasn't damaged or crushed. The Shrivers have absolutely no idea where it came from, for the desk had been cleaned and polished many times over the years, and the missing knob had never turned up. The house had been empty all winter, and employees who were with them when they found it vouch for the fact that the Shrivers didn't invent the story. The fifth pull has been screwed into place on the desk drawer, where it sits today.

The house ghost, poltergeist, gift horse, or whatever it might be, apparently has a cultural bent, for over the years, original copies of the musical *No, No, Nanette* (Mr. Shriver is related to lyricist Otto Harbach) and two slim volumes of *The Kings and Queens of France* have disappeared and just as inexplicably reappeared several weeks later in their places on the library shelf. The employees have never shown interest in these books, and Mr. and Mrs. Shriver are quite sure that they weren't playing tricks on each other. Both had noted this strange situation at different times, and neither found it amusing.

The only phenomenon that has been a constant is the ringing telephone in the Shrivers' bedroom. Every night just after midnight, the bedside phone gives three feeble chirps. They are shorter than a normal ring, and Mrs. Shriver described them as the kind of quick, anemic *brrt* sound sometimes heard from a phone during a big electrical storm. When the receiver is picked up, a regular dial tone is heard. If someone is using the phone at the time the chirping usually occurs, it functions normally. They have contacted the phone company several times to find out whether crossed lines, electrical surges, or some other mechanical foul-up could be responsible. The answer seems to be no.

The house on Main Street was built by John Gardner in the 1830s. The land had originally belonged to his great-umpteenth grandfather, Richard Gardner, in 1673. After John Gardner repurchased the family land in the early nineteenth century, it was passed from generation to generation. Shortly after the house was built, as the story goes, two Gardner brothers brought a Chinese houseboy back from a voyage. His presence on the island was probably un-usual enough for families to inquire about where he lived and whom he worked for. One day he simply disappeared. He had apparently overstepped his bounds with one of the Gardner sisters, whose brothers murdered the boy in a fit of rage. There are no papers to document the death, and the Gardner brothers were never brought to trial, but the story was recorded by several contempo-raries. It was said that the murder took place upstairs, in what later became the Shrivers' bedroom.

A Flying Candlestick

The house was built in 1785 on Center Street and was restored and divided into five small apartments in the 1960s. Larry Vienneau and Malcolm Barreiros shared one of the ground-floor apartments during the winter season of 1977 to '78. Larry is a painter, printmaker, and scrimshander; Malcolm was the chef at the India House for several years, and is now the *sous-chef* at the Second Story Restaurant.

The apartment was an ideal winter rental. It was cozy and warm, and was right in the middle of town. The combination of low, eighteenth-century ceilings, exposed beams, plastered walls, and original floorboards guaranteed that no surface was quite level and no line quite straight. The place seemed to toss and roll with a stubborn will of its own, and visitors were often thrown off balance in trying to navigate from room to room.

Malcolm had the smaller and darker of the bedrooms. Although freshly painted and scrubbed, the room had a sour, bitter smell to it when he arrived there. It had not improved any by the time he moved out. He tried leaving his window open for days on end, dragging the furniture out, washing the walls and floor, and even burning incense. The odor persisted. Malcolm's old dog would stick his head into the room when his master called him from inside, and then, blinking apologetically, would turn and slink back into the living room. Malcolm tried carrying him in and setting him down. The dog would scramble for the door, his tail between his legs. A cat stayed in the apartment for several weeks that winter, and she never willingly entered Malcolm's room either. When carried in, she would squirm and scratch and leap for the door.

Larry and Malcolm had an old stereo in the living room. Every so often, one of them would go to put on a record and find that the air just above and around the turntable was freezing cold. Anyone who happened to be in the apartment could run a hand in and out of the cold spot; it had definite boundaries, and could be felt even when the rest of the apartment was a comfortable 65 to 70 degrees. Malcolm says he remembers one morning when his girlfriend was staying for the weekend, and the entire living room suddenly felt like a walk-in freezer, but the thermostat registered a normal 65 degrees.

One December afternoon Larry was alone in the apartment, listening to the stereo while working on a piece of scrimshaw in his bedroom. He went into the living room to change a record and noticed that the cold spot above the turntable was back again. He didn't think much of it, crossed the room to the cabinet where he kept his albums, and was just bending over to pull one out when something very heavy hit the wall near his head with a sharp crack. He jumped up, his heart thudding. An oversized pewter candlestick that had come with the apartment was lying on the floor at his feet. The candlestick, which was kept on a table next to the stereo, had apparently flown diagonally across the room, a distance of about ten feet, and crashed next to Larry. It would have taken a strong arm to throw the candlestick that hard. Larry felt the hair rising on the back of his neck.

Malcolm arrived home ten minutes later, and when Larry told him what had happened, he laughed and just said, "Jesus, Larry, what's wrong? Long winter?" Going into the kitchen, Malcolm put the groceries down and started dinner. Larry was shaken, but he laughed too, and shrugged. Joining Malcolm in the kitchen, he picked up a towel to dry some of the dishes on the drainboard. He put the first plate down on the center of the table. As he turned his back for another, there was a loud crash. The first plate was in smithereens on the floor. As both men watched, Larry put a second plate down on the center of the table. The dish slid rapidly toward the edge, as if being pushed, and smashed on top of the first one.

As they stood there, incredulous, a long handmade nail flew out of the kitchen window frame and bounced onto the middle of the table. The nail was old, but in good condition. Had it simply fallen out, it would have landed on the sill below, but it had shot out of place, landing a good three feet from the window. Ten minutes later they heard the latch on the front door click down, and the door swung open of its own accord.

Malcolm and Larry ate out that night.

The foul smell in Malcolm's room and the periodic cold spot continued, but the men had no further trouble with objects flying and sliding of their own accord. Larry and Malcolm moved the candlestick down under the couch the next morning, where it stayed until they moved out the following May.

Miss Phebe Beadle

Rita Goss, of Main Street, is convinced that she shares her house with Miss Phebe Beadle.

"Miss Beadle had gone to Vassar, and she taught school on Nantucket for many years. She loved children, and was a warm, spontaneous kind of person. She lived in the house for eighteen years, from 1915 until her death in 1933. The schoolteacher was known to do unconventional, slightly risqué things; one Nantucketer told me, in a scandalized tone, that she was even seen sunbathing once or twice in her swimsuit on the widow's walk. I was delighted.

"Right after I bought the house, I had a strange experience. I had locked it up during the middle of the day and gone to do an errand. I returned to find the front door unlocked and slightly ajar. No one else on the island, that I knew of, had a key to the house. As I stepped in, I heard someone playing the piano. This was no faint tinkling of notes; it was the regular tone of someone at the keyboard. I was so startled that afterward I couldn't remember what the melody was, but I do remember that it was cheerful and pleasant-sounding.

"I stood for a moment in the doorway, wondering what I should do. Then, telling myself that on Nantucket the intruder couldn't be anyone too terrifying, I peeked around the corner to the parlor. As I did, the music stopped abruptly. The piano bench was vacant. When I got over my initial surprise, I walked through the entire house from room to room. Sure enough, I was alone.

"I asked around, trying to find out about the people who had lived there before me. The house was built about 1830 by a member of the Coffin family. Of course, no one now living could personally remember much about the people who owned the place before 1900, but of all the tenants I heard stories about, Miss Phebe Beadle sounded the most congenial. I have no idea who or what was really playing the piano, but I like to think it was she. Perhaps it was just her way of inviting me in, of telling me that I was welcome in her house."

A Red Friend

"I was living alone in the house, and slept in the downstairs bedroom. I was awakened one night by a brilliant red light shining across my bed. I thought perhaps there had been an accident on the road; the light looked like the red beam cast by a police car or ambulance."

Bill Armstrong is a painter and former resident of Nantucket who now lives in Manhattan. During the winter of 1976 he rented a house in Polpis that then belonged to Prentice Claflin. The Claflins had moved to a smaller house for the winter. In an even, dry tone, Bill continued:

"I got up and went to the window. I looked out. I looked away, closing my eyes, and then looked out again. There, standing on a little porch outside the house, was a woman. She was bright red. She looked the way someone does under a red spotlight on stage. She was solid, but I knew from the red glow of her body that she wasn't real. I mean, I knew she wasn't alive. I found myself thinking, as if in slow motion, 'She's a ghost. A red ghost. I'm seeing a red ghost of a woman.' I don't know why I wasn't terrified, but I felt quite calm. She was about forty years old, and was wearing conservative, simple clothing that I couldn't date. I noticed that her dress was dark, although I don't remember the length, and that she had dark hair. She stared right into my eyes. Her expression was impassive, emotionless. She wasn't tragic and she wasn't threatening. I didn't feel at all the way I would have expected to feel when looking at a ghost. After we had faced each other for something like a minute, she began to fade, becoming fainter and fainter, and finally vanished altogether. I got back into bed and went to sleep.

"I saw her three more times. She always appeared at night outside the house. She was outside my bedroom window every time but one, when I saw her standing out in back, near the driveway. She was dressed the same way each time, and always looked right at me. I came to think of her as, well, a watchful friend. Maybe it's just that I was living alone and knew that if I didn't simply accept her I'd be so terrified that I'd have to move out.

"There were three or four other times when I couldn't see her but knew she was in the house with me. Once, in the evening, I was watching television downstairs and began to hear the sounds of a party coming from the empty dining room. People were laughing and talking, and I could hear the clink of china and glasses. I got up and looked into the room, but, as I suspected, there was nothing visible going on. Not knowing what else to do, I tried to ignore it and went back to my program.

"One night I had just gotten into bed, and was lying there thinking, when suddenly I knew she was in the room with me. This is probably the strangest of all my encounters with her, for she sat down on the edge of the bed. I actually felt the bed go down under her weight, although I couldn't see her. I don't know what got into me, but after a few moments I held up the covers and said, 'All right, get in!' With that, she stood up and was gone.

"An odd thing happened one night when my ex-wife stayed in the library. I forget now why she did, but it was late, I had a bunch of guests in the house, and I remember her sleeping on the sofa in there. Prenny Claflin had an impressive collection of books which covered most of one wall. In the middle of the night, with no warning, the entire wall of books flew from the shelves and crashed on the floor. It woke us all up. It was violent and inexplicable. No person could ever have flung all those books out at once without knocking down the wall. My ex-wife and I were in the midst of a complicated divorce at that time, and some of my friends have since remarked that the red woman was probably commenting on my ex-wife's presence in the house.

"I told Patty and Prenny and various friends about the things that went on that winter, but the Claflins said that they had never felt or seen anything abnormal in the house. One night, as we were sitting around talking, someone suggested that we try a séance. None of us had had any experience with such things, but it sounded intriguing, so several nights later a bunch of us, including Patty Claflin and a musician named John Houshman, sat down around the dining-room table with a Ouija board. The first thing we did was to ask if someone was there. The answer was spelled right out: YES. I don't think we had really expected it to work. Our next question was whether she needed help. Again, the answer was YES. At that point Patty said she was beginning to feel uncomfortable, and she got up and went into the living room to sit by the fire. After she left, John also began to look nervous, and left to join Patty. The rest of us closed the door and continued.

"The next question we asked was, 'Is there anyone here who can help you?' The answer was spelled right out: BILL. At that point I began to feel funny, being the only Bill in the room, and decided it was time to break up the session. We talked about what had happened. I think we all felt a little shaky.

"We joined Patty and John, and I explained that the ghost had asked for help from 'Bill,' and that I had then gotten cold feet and put the Ouija board away for the night. Patty said, after a shocked pause, 'Well, we just heard her leave!' She and John had been absorbed in a conversation when they both heard a back door in the corner of the living room open and then slam shut. The door, in actuality, remained closed the entire time. They then heard footsteps clumping up what seemed to be a staircase running up the outside wall of the house. When the footsteps reached the second floor, Patty and John heard another door being yanked open and slammed shut. Both had sat, transfixed, listening to the sounds of the steps thumping diagonally up the outside wall. No stairs run up the outside of the house, and there is no door at the top opening onto the second floor. The house was built about 1830, and there is no structural indication of such a staircase or of such a door upstairs.

"And that's about it. My lease on the house ended soon after that, and I moved back to New York. I love Nantucket, but there were a few too many strange goings-on there. One only needs one such red friend in a lifetime."

Ancient History

"I don't have much to tell you, really. I'm the kind of person who just hates publicity and, quite honestly, I'd be glad if you didn't think this was enough of a story to write up. Well, let's see. What? You'll have to look right at me when you say something, because I hate using my hearing aid and seldom do.

"My husband and I bought the house thirty years ago. We knew that it had belonged to a woman who was very active in Nantucket politics during the American Revolution, but that was about the extent of our historical knowledge of the building. Some years ago I read up on all the details of her life, and she was quite a character, as you probably know. At any rate, we bought the house to enjoy and live in, and we've never dwelt on its background.

"Of course, what I'm going to tell you is all ancient history now; these things happened during our first couple of years in the house. I was staying here alone one summer with our two children; one was five, and one was still in a crib. My husband came home when he could on weekends.

"I wasn't the bravest soul in the world, at least not at that time, and although I never locked the house, I never quite relaxed, either. I was reading in bed one night when I heard a door slam. I froze and listened. I tried to read again, turning the pages quietly so as to hear—and, probably, so as not to be heard. Then I got a grip on myself, and said to myself firmly, 'Now, you're a grown woman with two little children. You should get up and check on that door, and close it if it has blown open.' So, rather timidly, I got up and walked out of my bedroom, through that door there, and into this room.

"I was standing a couple of feet from where you're sitting, right there at the edge of the rug, when I saw a woman walk through the dining-room door. She took a couple of steps and stopped opposite me. My first desperate thought was that it was some kind of optical illusion or shadow, or that a light outside was casting a strange reflection of my own body. I remember my neck went stiff as a board. I slowly turned my head, just a fraction of an inch, to see, with the corner of my eye, whether the shade was up on the window behind me. It wasn't. Besides, I was in pajamas and had curly, shoulder-length hair, and she was in a long skirt with her hair either short or pulled back in a bun. She was no reflection. I was absolutely rigid with terror. She was opaque; I couldn't see her features or the details of her shirt, but I could make out the shape of her head and the long skirt. I remember thinking that if I reached toward her I wouldn't be able to feel anything, that my hand would go through her. I suppose all this happened very quickly, but it seemed like it took forever. I was right next to a standing lamp, and I finally moved and switched the light on. As soon as I did, she disappeared. *Hooph!* It still gives me chills to talk about this.

"I told my husband about her, and of course he thought I was imagining things. He's a physicist, and the last person to believe in such an occurrence. One night, however, I had heard him rustling the covers and sighing and turning over heavily, but I didn't completely wake up. The next morning I asked him what had been wrong. He said in a grumpy voice, 'I saw your friend. She stood right in the doorway.'

" 'Oh!' I said. 'What did you do?'

" 'What in heck do you think? Turned over and went back to sleep!' He still hates to admit that he ever saw her, and will sometimes tell people, if it comes up in conversation, that he never did.

"A couple of other little things happened, but again, they're hardly spectacular and you might not want to write them up. One was that over there, by the fireplace, we had a stack of newspapers with an inverted metal bucket on top of it and two rubber toys on top of that. My five-year-old girl, who had a very matter-of-fact, direct approach to things, asked me when I went into her room one morning what all the rustling of papers in the living room the night before had been. I stuck my head into the living room and saw the oddest sight. The bucket and toys had been placed to one side of the fireplace, and the papers had been folded and set up, in sections, as little tents all over the room. So *that* was weird, but really rather silly.

"The only other thing that happened had to do with water. We had terribly rusty water in the house when we first moved in. For a couple of summers, all our white clothes turned beige or brown, the children's hair took on orange highlights, and I finally gave up and bought brown towels and sheets. Well, my little daughter called me one morning and said that the end of her bed was wet. I went into her room, and there was, indeed, a big rusty water spot on her bedspread. The window by the end of her bed was wide open, and the screen had been pulled all the way up. It looked as if someone had opened the window, yanked up the screen, and poured a bucket of our rusty water on the bed. That was when I went around the house and nailed down all the first-floor screens.

"So that's really all that happened. I'm afraid you've come all the way out here for nothing. Oh, yes, and we and our guests have heard footsteps clumping around upstairs quite a few times when there was no one up there. I always felt slightly embarrassed to have to explain to startled visitors that it was just the ghost."

A Smell of Roses

"It was in the winter of 1978 to '79 that all this happened. Now, I'm the kind of person who will find a rational explanation for an experience if it's at all possible, and I never pay any attention to the random bumps and creaks one always hears in an old Nantucket house. But I would describe what went on that winter as a prolonged exchange between me and something in the building.

"The house made me nervous. I felt that I had to let it know that I was friendly and uncritical, but that I wasn't about to let anything alarm me or push me out. I'm a firm believer in the idea that buildings do have personalities."

The young woman talking is an artist. She requested that her name not be used.

The house, in the center of town, is said to have been moved there from Capaum Pond around 1720. It was owned by Gardners, Barrens, Coffins, Mitchells, and Eastons, and has housed, among others, a mariner, a blockmaker, a cooper, two noted silversmiths, and a successful whaling merchant.

"I was living alone in the house that winter. I began to notice an occasional strong whiff of roses. It was a localized scent, as if I had walked right up to someone wearing rose cologne. The odor was sickly sweet and extremely concentrated. It was usually in one of the rooms downstairs, although I smelled it once in my bedroom.

"I can't tell you what a strange sensation it is to smell something as immediate and as heavy as rose perfume when there is no possible physical explanation for it. There was something horribly sweet and sentimental and old about it, something that brought to mind Dickens's Miss Haversham. I tried to be matter-of-fact about the scent and not let it scare me. But really! Imagine being alone in an eighteenth-century house on a windy February night and suddenly smelling roses from an invisible source. It wasn't easy. And it wasn't just me; friends visiting me at the house smelled it too. Occasionally, two or three people would be in one room, and we would all become aware of it. Sometimes it would be in one particular spot and someone would stumble into it, so to speak, and call the others. After several months, the smell, when it was present, seemed to be softening. It didn't have the same cloying intensity to it. I can't help thinking that my determination not to let it frighten me had something to do with its disappearance. It came less and less frequently, and finally stopped altogether.

"A funny thing once happened upstairs in my bedroom. I was sleeping one night when I was awakened by loud thumps and bumps. It sounded as if a large bird were flying around and flapping against the walls of the room. It was an agitated, frantic sound. I didn't get out of bed, but I could tell that there was nothing visible causing the noise. I think I said something that I hoped was soothing to the empty air, but the sounds continued. I remember hearing fire engines in town as I lay awake listening to the thumps. I fell asleep before the noise stopped, and found out the next morning that Zero Main Street had burned down in the night. It was one of the worst fires in an old Nantucket building in years. Perhaps there was some connection between the frantic sounds in my room and the fire, but I wouldn't know what it meant even if there were!

"I try to be sensible about all this. When you think of it, it would be strange if there were no human residue, no remnants of lives, in these old houses. Layers of living haven't been swept away here as they have in most modern communities; Nantucket is still quiet and isolated in the winter, and her history is her great strength.

"I think that the smell of roses and the flapping sound were something in the ongoing past of the house that I happened to bring out by my presence that winter. Something invisible was there and I was there, and we crossed paths."

Harry

"I did see Harry once. It was early June in 1974, and I was the first one in the family to get to the house that summer. My parents had bought Aloha a couple of years before, and I loved the place. I was looking forward to having a few days by myself. I was just seventeen. I remember that I opened a bottle of wine and sat down by the fireplace over here, right about where you're sitting, and smoked cigarettes and thought about life in general, and boys in particular, and felt pretty cool.

"There was a terrible storm that night, and buckets of rain were coming down. That porch wraps around three sides of the second story, as you can see. I was facing the porch door, and although I had a fire going it was dark inside. I was drowsy and starting to think about bed when something made me look up. I saw an older man peering in at me through the door. That porch is only accessible from inside the house."

Bonnie Block paused to help her one-year-old daughter with a cinnamon roll. It was Labor Day, and some of the Block family had gathered at Aloha for the weekend. Huntington T. Block is an insurance broker, and he and his wife, Amie, live in Washington, D.C. Their daughters, Bonnie and Amie, both live in New York City; Bonnie works for NBC in marketing, and Amie works in commercial real estate.

"Please have some coffee. Mom will be here in a minute. She's digging out our pictures of Harry. She can also tell you more about the history of the house than I can.

"So there I was, alone in the house, staring at this man outside the door. He was short and had a pleasant face. I can't picture his nose or eyes or mouth in any detail, but I do remember that he had a soft covering of some kind over his head, like the hood on a raincoat, and that he looked at me with a friendly, 'Well, here we are' expression. And then, suddenly, he just wasn't there. There was a big bang, and I saw a white flash on the edge of the porch up by the roof. Of course I panicked, thinking: Oh, great. Mom and Dad aren't here, I've set the house on fire, and there's a weirdo on the porch. *Now* what am I going to do?

"More afraid of the house burning down than of my visitor, I jumped up and jerked the door open. I stepped out on the porch. There was no man, and there was no fire—just plenty of darkness and lots of rain. I stood there for a moment trying to figure out what had happened. If the man had run off, I would have seen him through the windows. And the noise and the flash could have been thunder and lightning, but the storm was not an electrical one. I hurried inside, closed and locked all the doors, and started to feel a little less thrilled about being alone that night."

Amie, who had been listening to her sister's story, laughed. "That's amazing, Bonnie. Your experience and mine were so similar. We haven't talked about this in detail for ages."

Amie sat down on the sofa and blew on her coffee. She went on: "I was here early one spring with a friend from high school. Her name is Rachael Silin, and she lives on Nantucket year-round now. This incident must have happened two or three years after Bonnie saw Harry on the porch.

"It was a rainy evening, and I was sitting in the big chair over there. Rachael and I were gabbing away when we heard a tremendous crash that seemed to come from outside. Rachael glanced up first, and I saw her face drop. It was classic; I knew there was something awful out there. I turned and saw a short man, a perfectly solid figure. He was peeking in through the porch door. Rachael and I sat there for a moment, paralyzed, and then his little white face whooshed off to the left, and there was a funny scuttling noise, and he was gone.

"We were terrified. We would, if possible, have climbed on each other's laps. We had both seen someone out there, and that someone hadn't looked quite normal.

"I'm going to give Rachael a ring. I told her that you were coming over sometime this morning, and I know she'd be happy to give you her version of what happened."

Rachael introduced herself over the phone and started right in: "Oh, I remember it very clearly. I was sitting facing the porch door, and Amie and I heard a big bang, and suddenly I saw someone looking in. It was the face of an older man, say, someone in his late fifties, and it was very pale, kind of powdery. He was smiling. We could see something of his body, too; I remember shoulders. I just had time to register that I was seeing something pretty strange, and then he was gone, kind of flying off down one side of the porch. You could see him through the windows. He moved too quickly to have been running. We also heard a scrabbling sound.

"When Amie and I finally felt brave enough to investigate, we clutched each other and went around the entire porch. There was no one in sight. As there aren't any outside stairs to the second story, he couldn't have gotten down without jumping. And, anyway, he didn't look like someone who *could* have jumped; he didn't look quite real. I don't know how Amie feels about it now, but just thinking about seeing that little white face still gives me the absolute creeps."

After I had hung up, Bonnie returned to the living room. "The oddest run-in with Harry, that we know of, concerned a teenager by the name of Gary Rice," she began. "This also happened years ago. He was a friend of a friend, and he had nowhere to stay. It was his first visit to Nantucket. We offered to let him sleep up in the attic for a night. Our attic is almost like a loft; it has several beds and has always been used for spillover sleeping space.

"My two brothers and my sister Amie and I were all sitting around the kitchen table when Gary came downstairs in the morning. He was kind of quiet, helped himself to juice and some coffee, and then blurted out, 'Boy, the weirdest thing happened last night. I don't think it was a dream. I was asleep, and I woke up to see this guy standing next to my bed. He said, in a very formal, old-fashioned way, "Hello, I'm Harry Woodruff. I'm sorry to have woken you." That was the only thing he said. He spoke very clearly. Then he turned and walked off into one of the storage rooms and closed the door. I waited a moment, and then got up and followed him. I was pretty sure that there was no one upstairs with me. It was pitch black. I found the light and turned it on. The room was empty except for some old furniture and a pile of boxes.'

"Amie and I looked at each other, and said, 'Okay! Stop the b.s.! Who told you?' Gary honestly didn't know what we were talking about. We had some of Harry's memorabilia in a drawer, and one of us went and got a handful of photographs of Harry and brought them into the kitchen. At the time, we had no pictures of him hanging in the house. Gary was floored: 'Jesus! There he is. *There he is*. He looks younger here, but this is definitely the same man. You've got to be kidding.' He was incredulous about having seen this Harry character in the attic in the middle of the night. And he was upset. I never got to know Gary very well, but I'll call someone who was a close friend of his and see if I can track him down for you. I think he's living in New Jersey now."

Mrs. Block came into the room carrying a shoebox and several large framed photographs. "Oh, that Gary business! Wasn't that just wild? Hello, my dear. You can spread these out on the table here.

"His stage name was Harry Meredith, but his given name was Henry Meredith Woodruff. We've always called him Harry Woodruff, I guess because that's what he was known by in 'Sconset. He was enamored of Hawaii, and he built this house along the lines of a classic Hawaiian dwelling and named it Aloha. The name isn't one we would have chosen, but we could hardly change it after so many years. At any rate, Harry moved in in 1904 with a Filipino manservant."

Mrs. Block passed me a framed photograph of Harry. It is a coffee-colored sepia, in profile, of a young man. Resplendent in a skintight tunic, a helmet, soft leather boots, and shin guards, he looks as though he might have stepped out of a production of *Julius Caesar*. There are photographs of "Mr. Harry Meredith" as Charles the Wrestler (according to the inscription) and Robin Hood. He appears in numerous publicity shots; he is standing, sitting, in profile, straight on. He appears in capes, in leotards, in fur. There is something of the young Paul Newman's sensuous, limpid gaze in these portraits of Mr. Harry—he had full lips, a chiseled nose, and sleepy, come-hither eyes.

Based in New York City, Harry played Broadway and toured the United States. He also did summer stock. Margaret Faucett Barnes, in her 1969 memoir, '*Sconset Heyday*, describes Harry Woodruff as "a handsome man with wavy blond hair who could charm the women across the footlights without even half trying." She also remembers visiting Aloha as a child: "After a season of acting in Honolulu, Harry Woodruff brought back from the Pacific Island a plan of a house which was built for him on his beloved island in the Atlantic Ocean. With bedrooms downstairs, the whole of the upstairs was a large living-dining room, with only a corner partitioned off for a kitchen, and surrounded on three sides by a wide porch. Being a most hospitable man he had gatherings of friends . . . who filled these porches, exchanging bits of theatrical gossip interspersed with exclamations about the view of sea and moors and sunsets."

Siasconset, a village made up of cod-fishing shacks on the east shore of Nantucket, became a haven for artists and actors during the last years of the nineteenth century. With no air conditioning, urban theater came to a halt during the summer months, and actors went on tour or looked for a place to stay in the country. Word got out that 'Sconset was affordable and unspoiled. By 1900, the Actors' Colony, as it came to be known, was a busy spot from June to September.

Harry Woodruff became a familiar presence. He built his house shortly after the turn of the century, and was to sell it twelve years later, in 1916. By then the promise of year-round employment in Hollywood drew many professionals away from the East Coast circuit, and the advent of air conditioning kept theaters open during even the hottest months. Actors no longer had an excuse to come to Nantucket every summer, and the colony dwindled.

Harry sold the house and "one acre, 152½ rods of land" to Sarah Johnson Hutton of Cincinnati. Five generations of Huttons were to use the house.

Elizabeth Hutton Timpson related the following: "I'm eighty-four. When my parents bought Aloha, it was full of the most extraordinary things.

"There were a number of huge Samoan *tapa* cloths hanging on the walls. They were just fantastic, made out of some kind of bark and covered with animals and geometric designs. I believe that my great-niece, Inez Hutton, took one with horses to the Museum of Natural History in New York, and Margaret Mead came down from her offices to take a look at it. Everyone agreed that it was quite a treasure.

"I can remember two things in particular about our first summer in the house. First of all, it looked as if Harry had just stepped out for a walk. He seemed to have left almost all of his personal possessions behind. There was a standing screen with burlap panels that divided the kitchen area from the main part of the second-floor living room. That screen was absolutely covered with photographs of actors and actresses who had been friends of his. Of course, these days no one has even heard of him, but in that era Harry Woodruff was a respected name on the stage. My parents recognized almost all of the faces in Harry's collection, and I can remember them exclaiming as they pored over those photographs.

"My other memory had to do with wine. There were dozens of Chianti bottles hanging in clusters from the ceiling. Chianti came with a straw case around the decanter, and he had looped all of the bottles up by their handles. A couple of them still had a splash of wine in the bottom. I have a memory of my father muttering as he grappled with the bottles; he was not pleased when his shirtfront got covered with vinegar.

"Harry was a very gregarious fellow, and everybody in 'Sconset loved him.

I think he was also a kind person. He used to visit the elderly Nantucketers at Our Island Home, and he got very attached to one aging sea captain, a certain Billy Bowen. Harry built a little two-room cottage on the front of his property, and he moved Billy in and had his Filipino servant cook food for him and carry three meals a day across the lawn.

"And Harry was eccentric. He brought the same three bachelors to the house with him every summer, men who were also in the theater, and they stayed up all night and slept all day. I can remember extremely heavy curtains over all the bedroom windows.

"Harry deeply loved Nantucket and was very attached to his unusual island home. I remember hearing that he died shortly after we moved in. My parents talked about his death in a hush-hush way, and I suppose I was too young to hear the details. I think Harry either lost all his money or became quite ill. At any rate, he'd sold his beloved Aloha because he had to. My parents felt rather bad about that."

Sarah Hutton:

"I'm a jeweler, and I'm living year-round on Nantucket now. Let's see . . . Aloha. It was a very special place, not like any other house I'd ever been in. It was different physically, being the first upside-down house (bedrooms on the first floor, living room on the second) to be built on Nantucket, and it was different in feeling. The building has a dramatic, wide-open look that is a change from the modest lines of a saltbox or a lean-to. When my great-grandmother, Sarah J., moved into the house, there were trunks full of costumes and all kinds of theater memorabilia; I can remember, even in my day, seeing piles of faded photographs of Harry and of his friends, and programs from productions he had been in. I can't imagine why he left so many of his personal things behind, but, whatever the reason, there they were. The Huttons moved most of his clothing and papers up to the attic, and we kids had a wonderful time exploring.

"There were bunks along the walls of the main room in the attic, and the grandchildren all slept up there. I must have been about ten when I first heard Harry; at least, we assumed it was Harry. I was awakened one very dark night by the sound of someone walking around in the separate storage space where Harry's things were kept. I could hear trunks being opened and closed and papers rustling. It was unmistakable; there was a person, an adult, busily rummaging around under the eaves. I was so terrified that I held my breath as long as I possibly could, for fear of being heard, and I can remember, to this day, thinking that my heart sounded like thunder. I was so afraid that whoever was in there might come out and see me that I didn't dare wake anyone or get up. I couldn't sleep until long after the noises had stopped. Of course, no one came out. I heard someone poking around on several other occasions, always at night, and always when I was the only one awake. None of the other kids, as far as I know, heard anyone up there. I most definitely did.

"My cousin Inez lives out here, and she spent quite a bit of time alone in the house as an adult. You should give her a call."

Inez Hutton:

"I was twenty-five when I spent a summer alone at Aloha. It was 1971, shortly before the house was sold to the Blocks. I slept up on the second floor, on the *hikiee*; it was a Hawaiian structure, a generous built-in couch in the corner that could be used for naps or just stretching out after a meal. It would have felt lonely to sleep downstairs, and besides, the sunrises and early morning light in the living room are just marvelous.

"I had no television, and I used to do a lot of crewel work at night. I was often up until 1:00 or 2:00 A.M. The first time I heard him was in the spring, shortly after I had moved in. It was well after midnight. I can remember that it was very quiet and peaceful in the house, and my three cats were asleep in the living room. I was in one of the armchairs, stitching away, and I heard someone walk across the attic floor above me. I stopped. Someone walked back the other way. And back again. An adult was pacing, in street shoes, on the wooden floor. I can remember looking up and following the sound along the ceiling.

"The first time I heard it, it really did shake me up. We had all joked about Harry, but can you imagine being alone in a house in 'Sconset, out in the boonies, and hearing another person walking around? I sat and listened for three or four minutes. And then, to my relief, the pacing stopped abruptly. My cats never even stirred.

"This wasn't a one-shot thing. I heard Harry maybe twenty times. The circumstances were always similar: I was alone, it was early, early morning, and I was still fully dressed and awake. And it never happened on crystal-clear nights; it always seemed to be foggy or rainy weather. I heard him in the spring and in the fall; I don't remember hearing him in July or August.

"My cats were never disturbed by the sound, even when they were sitting up or moving around. I found this reassuring; animals are a pretty good barometer of anything unpleasant or malevolent lingering in a house. In fact, I had a German shepherd staying with me for several weeks, and the attic pacing started up late one night while the dog was in the house. He got up and walked slowly to the foot of the ladder and looked up into the dark. He whined a little and put his paws up on the bottom rung. There were no hackles or growls. He simply stood there, looking up into the darkness, listening to the pacing. He then dropped down and walked away. I knew, at that point, that Harry was an okay guy.

"I did force myself to climb up into the attic one night and turn on the light. The pacing stopped as soon as I started up the ladder. When I got to the top, the attic was empty."

A Pink Rocker

"Dev and I used to take in boarders in the summer. Most of them slept in the room with the pink rocker.

"We had this one boy, Alex, who came for three or four days every August. The last time he stayed with us was in 1979, while he was a student in law school. He appeared at the breakfast table on his last morning here and said, 'Mrs. Dev' (that's what they used to call me), 'is this house haunted?'

" 'Well, of course it is, Alex!' I said.

" 'There was a woman in my room last night, sitting in the pink rocker. She was very thin and had straight black hair, some of it piled up in a knot, and very sharp features. She had a long, old-fashioned kind of print dress.' Alex described her in great detail.

"I said, 'Alex, are you sure you weren't looking at a pile of clothes on that chair?' He said no, the moon was bright and the sky clear, and he woke up and found her just sitting there looking at him. He looked at her, and she looked right back. That went on for a few minutes. Then he said he turned on the light and the chair was empty. No clothes on it or nothing. Alex was very upset about it. He left on the boat that afternoon, and he never came back to stay with us. No, he never did come back.

"Now, I had an aunt who moved off-island when she was quite young. Her name was Aunt Susie. My father didn't like to talk about her, and my sister and I never knew why. At any rate, when she died in Williamstown, she left me some money. I was surprised; I didn't remember meeting her, even after my father was gone, and I never tried to visit or get in touch with her. I feel bad about that now. When I talked to the woman who took care of her, I said,

'Well, what did Aunt Susie look like?' and she said, 'Oh, she was thin and had a very angular-like face, and when she was young she had dark hair.' *Hooo*—of course I remembered what Alex had told me, and I got chills. He saw that woman in the chair around the same time that Aunt Susie died.

"A few odd things have gone on in the room with the pink rocker. David Hessler's daughter, Mary, stayed there when she was seventeen or eighteen, before she went into the Navy. She came down one morning and said, 'Oh, my God, Mrs. Dev! A big man tried to strangle me last night. He had his hands on my throat. It was real, Mrs. Dev. It was real.' She was absolutely sincere. I tried to tell her it was probably a nightmare, but she wouldn't listen. She was pretty shook up.

"I didn't give it too much thought until some time later when we had two workmen sleeping in that same room. Chris and John were brothers, and were doing some renovation and painting in one of the churches. They had come from off-island—from Hingham or some such place—to do the job. On the morning after their first night in the house, John came into the kitchen and said to Dev and me, 'This damn house is haunted!' His brother said, 'That weren't no ghost! That was a plain old nightmare.' But John was very clear about it, and said, 'That was *no nightmare*. I woke up, and a big man was standing over me, and he was trying to strangle me. He had his hands on my damn throat. I let out a couple of war whoops, and he vanished. I'm gonna take a damn great stick to bed with me tonight!' I don't think he had any more trouble, but I think he slept with some kind of broom or something under the covers and the reading light on. The funny thing is that he had real red hair like Mary. His brother Chris had dark hair.

"Come on up and see the room. Dev's always wanted to replace these stairs, but I say, 'No, no, leave them the way they are. I'm attached to them, you know, and they work just fine.' My father bought this house in 1917, and I was born here. Actually, I was born half here and half in the hospital on Westchester Street, because it was what's called a 'difficult' birth.

"My mother died when I was fourteen, my sister left home, and I stayed and took care of my father. Then Dev and I met and were married, and we brought up our son, Nathan, here. This is the only house I've ever lived in.

"When I was growing up, we were the only house on this rise. There was a nice big field out behind us, and cows and wildflowers and all, and it was real pretty. Everybody's so elbow-to-elbow around here now, you feel like you're in the middle of a crowd. When I was a teenager I could look out this bedroom window and see between the houses to the corner of those two streets. That's quite a way. If there was a parade or something special going on, we could see them coming our way. I could also keep an eye out and see if one of my boyfriends was coming, and run and put on lipstick and do my hair before he got here. We used to have all kinds of peek-around places like that, goddamn it, and all the building has ruined those little views between things.

"We also used to have lots of neighborhood stores up this way. Where Fred Meadows's garage is now there was a candy store, and there was a bakery down the hill. We all went different places for different things: you'd go one place for buttons and thread, another place for soap, another for eggs, and so on. At the Monument Square Grocery they had a box for kids to stand on so they could see into the case, and my sister and I used to be able to get about ten different pieces of candy for a penny.

"Twenty years ago, a neighborhood was really made up of neighbors. There was a feeling of allegiance, of belonging. One of my neighbors, Mrs. J., was quick-tempered, and I am too. Well, she and I used to have these blow-ups once in a while, and we'd both go yammer-yammer-yammer at each other and turn around and march off into our houses. A few days later she'd come in the back door with a homemade lemon meringue pie or a coconut cream pie—she knew I loved both of those—and plop it down on the table and say, 'Here! This is for you,' real rough-like. Well, we'd sit down and have tea and a piece of her pie and start talking, and pretty soon everything would be okay, but neither one of us ever said we were sorry. No, I don't bend easily, and she didn't bend either, and we were like two fighting dogs when we got going, but we were always quick to help each other when there was trouble.

"Here's the room. It's the attic. Dev and I put in this wall and the bathroom. You can see the name L. M. Macy written on this rafter here, and the date 1877. The house is much earlier than that, but Macy probably did some work on the roof that year. We figure that the house is late 1700s. See these grooves in the overhead beam? That's where my father put up a swing for me. He had to move it a couple of times. Over on the other side, near the stairs, that's where my sister's swing was. We really wore the wood down. It was nice, because you could swing and swing and look out into the trees.

"Over here by the window is where the pink rocker was sitting when Alex stayed here. I had a boarder, a big guy, who sat in it and cracked it a few years ago, and it's since gone to the dump. Alex was sleeping in this bed, which was—now, let's see—only about twelve feet from the rocker. He was so sure about seeing that woman sitting there in the light of the moon.

"I don't mind her in the house, but I'm not wild about the big guy who went after Mary and John. But Dev and I don't interfere with whatever is here. They could be people who lived in the house before my family moved in. We accept whatever goes on, of that kind of spirit stuff, and leave it alone.

"Come on down. Watch your step. We've seen a couple of odd things in this family room. We spend most of our time here; there's the TV and the radio and our books. I usually sit in this chair here, and Dev sits there. We see the latch on the dining-room door right here going up and down. That happens quite a lot. Sometimes it'll make a helluva racket, and you can see that no latch would do that unless someone was pressing and then releasing it. No, I've never gone and opened the door when that's going on.

"Sometimes when we're watching TV the latch will go up and down real quiet and gentle-like, as if they were trying not to disturb us. My son, Nathan, has also been in the room when the latch started carrying on by itself.

"The only unpleasant thing Dev and I have seen in the house had to do with a little beagle we had for years. Scarlet was a very lovable, low-key dog, and we only saw her act real hostile on one occasion. We were sitting here one evening, reading magazines or chatting or something, and Scarlet suddenly jumped to her feet and backed up right against the sofa. She was growling and baring her teeth, and the hair was standing up on her back. She was facing the door with the restless latch, looking up at something which was about the height of a person. Dev and I couldn't see what was troubling her. Dev said, 'Chrissakes, Scarlet! What's the matter? Lie down—that's a good dog!' She didn't pay any attention. Then she slowly followed something, with her eyes, as it went around Dev's chair and all the way to the end of the room by the TV. And then Scarlet suddenly quieted down, plopped back on the rug, and acted normal again. As soon as whatever she had seen was out of the room, she felt fine.

"Lots of little things crop up in the old houses here, but people really don't like to talk about it. They'll admit it in passing, but then they don't want to think about it too much. The other day Dev and I were in my grandmother's house, right across the street. It just changed hands, and the fellow who was renovating it invited us in for a look. He did a terrible job. There were beautiful, wide, two-hundred-year-old floorboards that still had the original mill marks on them and had been spatter-painted by the last owner. All they needed was a good washing and waxing. Well, he had sanded them way down, and now they just look like new wood. And my grandmother had a fireplace with blue delft tiles all around it that he smashed and threw away.

"Anyway, as we were leaving he said, 'There's something funny in this place.' I said, 'Now, what do you mean?' He said, 'I don't know. Doors banging shut, footsteps on the second floor. We hear sounds of people up there when the whole crew is downstairs.' I said, 'Well, Chrissakes. Look what you've done! I'd probably slam doors too, if it'd been my house.' "

In the Window

The house sits on the top of a small hill off Orange Street. Close by are a gas station, a liquor store, a video rental outlet, a Cumberland Farms; the area along the road is zoned commercial, and businesses are beginning to take over what was once a sleepy, open stretch of land on the edge of town.

"When we first came out here, thirty years ago, we were looking for a summer rental and spotted this house. It was a little run-down, but looked intriguing. We asked around, and found out that the owner was ill and wouldn't be coming to the island that year. Her nephew agreed to rent us the house. We bought it shortly thereafter, furnished, for $8,500."

Andy Oates owns Nantucket Looms, on Main Street, with his partner, Bill Euler. Andy had an art gallery and framing business in Cambridge, Massachusetts, before he and Bill opened the Looms, a store specializing in fine hand-woven rugs and clothing, in 1968. Andy went on:

"The house was built somewhere around 1720, and we believe that it was a Bunker house. It was built on one of the so-called Fish Lots. Of course it could have been moved; it's very hard to tell exactly what went on with a building when you get back that far, for the records in the Registry of Deeds are concerned primarily with land transfers. Buildings were mentioned, but a building that was relocated is hard to trace.

"This is a classic half-house from that period. We have tried to preserve as much of the original plaster as possible (you know, they often mixed horsehair into the compound), and of course we have this wonderful big fireplace. There was a baking oven on one side, which we have turned into a closet, and there is still a root cellar under the floor. There used to be a trapdoor right where I'm standing. Most of the woodwork in the old part of the house is original, and in pretty good condition. As you can see, the rooms have all settled at different angles.

"We added the rest of the house. The original building was terribly small, and we needed more space. And of course it's much warmer in the addition during the winter; heating the old part was a little like heating the inside of a sieve.

"Shall we sit down? There really isn't too much to say here on the subject of ghosts. I've never seen anything in the house, and Bill says he isn't a believer, but he did have an odd experience about twenty-five years ago. He was outside cutting the grass on the upper lawn, and he glanced up at the side of the house and saw what looked like a woman's figure in the bedroom window. The curtain was pulled aside and then dropped. He says it all happened very quickly, and that it was probably a figment of his imagination.

"About ten years later, when we hadn't even thought about this little occurrence in years, a funny thing happened. A friend of ours came by when we were out. She was with her father, who was quite elderly and had just had a stroke. He stayed in the car, and she went to the kitchen door and knocked. I guess she opened the door and called to us, and when nobody answered, she went to the car. Her father, who was only able to say, 'yes,' 'no,' and a few other words, pointed to the bedroom window upstairs and said, 'Yes! Yes!' with great insistence. His daughter asked him if he had seen someone, and he nodded and pointed again. She went back and opened the door and called out to us once more. No one answered, and she returned to the car. Apparently he gestured to the upstairs window again, nodding emphatically, and got quite angry at her when she explained that she had already been in the house and that no one was home. He was very put out when she started up the car and left.

"When she mentioned it to us later, we were all rather surprised when we realized that it was the same window where Bill had (or hadn't) seen the woman.

"We've had friends stay in the house when we were gone. Richard Dannhauser claims that he had an absolutely hair-raising time when he was here alone, and a young woman who was staying here one winter heard so many strange noises in the house that she finally called my niece and said she couldn't possibly sleep here another night.

"I have never seen a ghost, but I have felt a kind of presence at the top of the back stairs and in the bedroom. At times the feeling is quite strong, but of course, it might just be my mood or the weather."

Richard Dannhauser, the owner of Orange Street Video, related the following: "I stayed in the house and took care of the cats for a couple of weeks one winter when Andy and Bill were away. My first ten days there were perfectly comfortable; I puttered around and did my own thing and went to bed early every night. Then, a few days before I left, I invited some friends over for dinner. We sat around the table talking until quite late. After everyone had gone, I was in the kitchen clearing up when I noticed something strange.

"I glanced through the French doors, which lead to the oldest part of the house, and saw that the latch door between the living room and the outer sitting room was open. I hadn't been using that wing of the house at all. I put down the dish I was holding, opened up the French doors, and walked over and closed the living-room door. It was very cold in there, so I hurried back into the kitchen and closed the French doors tightly behind me. About ten minutes later, I looked back in toward the living room. I was really surprised to see that the door was wide open again. In fact, I got kind of a sick feeling in the pit of my stomach; I *knew* I had closed that door firmly, and it had been shut all week. I dried my hands and marched back in through the sitting room and closed the door with a bang and locked it.

"Several minutes later I looked back in and the door was wide open again. I repeated the locking procedure. The door opened again by itself. That did it: I locked the French doors, turned out the kitchen light, and went to bed. The next day I went in and closed the rebellious door, and it stayed that way for the rest of my visit. However, I must say that I didn't sleep well that night or the following nights, and I couldn't wait to get out of the house. The cats and I were glad to see Andy and Bill."

You Wanted to See Me

"We rented an old house off Main Street in 1984. We were there for almost a year. On our first night in the house, my husband, Jesse, was in the bathtub and I was in bed, and I heard him muttering something in a quiet voice. I said, 'What are you saying?' He answered, 'Nothing.' I heard a voice again. I repeated the question, and he said, 'Nothing! I haven't opened my mouth. There's somebody talking.' We both listened, and sure enough, we could hear what sounded like two women having a conversation. It was a muffled noise, the way voices sound at a party when you're listening from another room. The talking seemed to be coming from the kitchen. We heard those same women chatting in a low, easy tone many times, but if you tried to track down the sound, it would fade away. You couldn't understand individual words, but you could pick up the general feeling of what they were saying."

Sarah Coffin works at Together, a clothing store on Main Street. Although she wasn't born on the island, her father is a native Nantucketer and a member of the Coffin family, and her parents moved back to the island with their five children when Sarah was six. She went through the Nantucket school system, left for college, and lived in Boston for a short time after she graduated. She returned to Nantucket and married Jesse Eldridge, who also grew up here, in 1983. Sarah went on:

"Those women talking were just the beginning. When Jesse's mother passed away, I came home alone after the funeral and was writing a letter in the living room when I heard a man's voice. It sounded like it was coming out of the bedroom. I said, 'Jess?'—knowing that it couldn't be him but feeling kind of confused. Nobody answered. I looked around the house, and no one was there but me. I told my husband, and then didn't think about it much until one night a couple of weeks later.

"We were asleep in bed, and it was late. Something woke me up, and I found that I couldn't move. And I mean *couldn't move*. It felt just like someone heavy was lying on top of me. I was on my back, with my arms stretched over my head and my face turned to the side. When I tried to call out, I couldn't speak or even open my mouth. I was literally paralyzed, and I can remember my heart began to pound, and I could feel the adrenaline flowing. I said, in my head, as fiercely as I could, 'Get off of me! Get off of me!' It worked; whatever it was got up and went away and I was able to speak and move again. Of course, I woke up Jesse in an absolute panic and couldn't settle down for a long time afterward. And from that night on, I could hear someone walking around in the attic over our bedroom. I would hear it now and then, not all the time; it was a shuffle, but it was definitely the sound of a person walking, in their shoes, on wood. I remember that the ceiling in our bedroom was bowed, and that I'd lie in bed and look up at it, wondering who could be up there. And I also remember hoping that whoever it was would stay right where they were. I wasn't too thrilled about the idea of another visit.

"One night Jesse was in the living room and I had just gone to bed. I wasn't asleep yet. (It sounds like I was always in bed, doesn't it?) Some mice had gotten into the house, and Jesse was laying traps. All the lights were on except for those in the bedroom. I looked over and saw a man standing in the bedroom door, facing me. He was absolutely still. I sat up in bed and said, 'Forget the mice, honey. We'll get them tomorrow,' but even as I was speaking, I realized that it wasn't Jesse. This man had on tan pants and a pale orange T-shirt. I couldn't see his features very well because the light was coming from behind him. Jesse said, 'What?' from back in the next room, and I kind of shook my head and looked again, and the figure was gone.

"Now, that was a strange experience, but not a particularly scary one; whoever it was hadn't bothered me. Jesse and I began to joke about charging our company rent.

"Sometime later I was in the house alone one night, and I was upset about something. I guess I was crying. I distinctly heard a woman's voice saying out loud, 'Ssh. Ssh. Don't cry,' over and over. It was so surprising that I stopped. Bonnie Fitzgibbon, who lived with us for a couple of months that winter, told me that she also heard the women talking when she was alone in the house. For some reason, I always felt that they were sisters chatting. The sound of the women was kind of nice.

"What happened next was not so nice. After the following incident, I was careful never to be in the house alone again, and we moved out several weeks later.

"It was about 2:00 A.M. I woke up thirsty, so I got out of bed and went to the kitchen to get something to drink. I was nude, and as I stood by the open door to the refrigerator, I suddenly had a creepy feeling that someone was watching me. I glanced quickly around the kitchen, and it was quite empty. After pouring myself some soda, I walked back to the bedroom.

"A minute or two later, I was sitting up in bed finishing my drink when I got an eerie something's-going-to-happen feeling. I can remember my scalp tightening. Then the bedroom door flew open, really fast and without a sound, and I saw an older man in the doorway. He had white hair and a beard and very bushy eyebrows, and was wearing a big baggy thing like a fisherman's sweater. He was kind of an outline—he was blurry at the edges—but I could see his shape and the coloration of his clothes. He was there in the doorway one moment, and then *whoosh!* he was right up in front of my nose. I can't tell you how terrifying that was. He moved with terrific speed, faster than anyone living ever could. Just inches from my face, he said, 'You wanted to see me so here I am!' Those were the exact words. And I knew his presence was evil. It may sound funny, but he was not a good person, and that was no friendly visit. I can still hear those words, and the way he said them: 'You wanted to see me, so here I am!' I don't know if I have ever been as scared. I hate to even talk about it. And I will never forget that face.

"After saying that, he vanished, and of course I shook Jesse and woke him up. My husband was pretty matter-of-fact about what happened, and said, 'He what?' and rolled over and went back to sleep. I can't blame him; it does sound pretty wild.

"I went to pay rent at the owner's house about a week later, and I told her that I felt sure our house had ghosts. She laughed and said, 'Well, that's what I've heard, but I don't believe in them.' Then I happened to look over at the mantel, where she had a bunch of framed snapshots, and there he was, standing on the beach with a fishing pole. Before I could stop myself, I said, 'That's the man I saw! That's him!' 'Oh, he died about eight years ago,' the owner replied. She told me calmly that he was either her father or her uncle, I can't remember which, and then she changed the subject. The house had been his.

"I've had one other very strange experience connected with an old house on the island. A few months before Jesse and I were married, I began having a recurrent dream. In the dream, I was walking through an incredibly beautiful, peaceful house. I would wander from room to room, and I felt really happy, just filled with warmth and a sense of belonging and fulfillment. It was a big house, with formal furniture and rugs, and I knew, somehow, that it was on Nantucket. And at the end of every dream, I found myself in a hidden room, looking down through a small interior window at a woman sitting below me. She was in Victorian clothing. Her dress was cut fairly low, and it had a tight, fitted bodice and generous floor-length skirts. She had dark hair, and her face wasn't visible from where I was standing. She was looking out a window at a pool, or at water. And in every dream, no matter where I went in the house, I could never find the door to the room she was sitting in.

"Those dreams were disturbing because they were so powerful. It wasn't that my real, everyday life wasn't happy, because it was, but I just felt that I *belonged* in that house. I had such a sense of peace and calm in those dreams. I would wake up disoriented, and it took me a while to shake off that other world; in fact, I really thought I might be going crazy. The dreams were not like the normal dream state. They gripped me. In the last one I had, I was standing outside the house and suddenly knew that I was the woman in the chair. I had been watching myself.

"A week later, in the *Inquirer and Mirror*, I saw the house. I remember sitting at the kitchen table and just staring at that photograph. The property was for sale, and it was described as a Coffin house. I called up the owner and asked her if Jesse and I could come and see it.

"We went in, and I knew where every room was. The furnishings were different, but I knew the entire layout. We went upstairs, and I asked the owner if we could go in to the secret room. She was a little surprised but she took us in, and sure enough, there was the little window and the room below. She explained that the lower room had been an addition to the original building. We left the hidden room and went down into the addition, and I went over to the corner where the woman had been sitting. The window she had been looking through was stained glass. It had a water scene on it, complete with tiny, delicate waves; here was the pool in my dream.

"After we visited the house my dreams stopped, and I thought that was an end to the whole thing.

"We got married September 24. Chick Walsh, who was Jesse's best man, had asked us where we'd like to stay on our wedding night. I told him that we'd like to be in a luxurious old house where we could have breakfast in bed. Chick gave us that night away from home as a present, and he wouldn't tell us ahead of time where we were going. When we found out, Jesse and I just looked at each other and laughed. The owner was a friend of Chick's, but aside from that, I have no idea what made him choose that particular place. No one but Jesse and I knew about my bizarre series of dreams. I was a little nervous about staying there, but as it turned out, I had a peaceful, dreamless sleep that night, a really heavenly sleep. After all, I guess I was home."

Three Fishermen

"You'll have to give me a few minutes to unwind, because it's been a horrendous afternoon. I usually go right home after work and soak in the tub." Seated on the patio of the Boarding House Restaurant, Shirley Ferguson looked up at the late July light drifting down through the elm leaves. "I can't believe it. This is the first time I've really noticed the sky all day. Let's see; I'll have a Perrier with two slices of lime, please.

"I'm a real estate broker, and my husband, Gregory, and I moved to the island in 1976. I bought our house in 1978. I had been looking for an old Nantucket house for a couple of years and hadn't seen anything that I really liked. I picked up a copy of *The Boston Globe* one day, something I never do, and flipped through the paper to the real estate listings. There, to my surprise, was a Nantucket house that I hadn't realized was on the market. I called up the owners, mostly out of curiosity, and went to take a look that afternoon.

"When I walked in, I knew immediately. I just knew from the moment I saw the place that this was it. It's funny how these things work. I had a terrible time actually purchasing the property, though. I had called up the people who were renovating a large house right next door because I knew that they owned commercial properties down the block; I wanted to find out if they were setting up a guesthouse or an annex to their business. That was a big mistake. They hadn't known until I contacted them that the house was for sale. By the time I called with an offer on the house that evening, the abutters had already bought it. I was devastated. I couldn't believe I had finally found a house I really loved only to have it snatched from under my nose. I ended up buying the house from the abutter for a considerably higher amount than the original asking price, but I would have done a lot more to get that building.

"Our house was built sometime before 1750. The Great Fire of 1848 stopped one house short of mine, which is why it is so much older than the buildings on the south end of the street. Interestingly enough, the house has changed hands many times. I think we've had it as long as any other single owner, and that's surprising, because in the nineteenth century, homes often passed from generation to generation. Maybe the building made people uncomfortable.

"The house is what you might call active. Unexplained things have gone on from the day we moved in. We've gotten to know how the house works, and we can sometimes predict a flare-up; it will be busy, for instance, a few days before and after a full moon, or when our children and their friends are home visiting. Things happen year-round, but I do notice more 'paranormal' shenanigans during the winter months.

"We hear lots of noises. The house is full of muffled voices and the sounds of people moving around. We hear laughing and giggling and singing, particularly on the second floor and in the attic. We can also hear the scampering sound of children's feet going back and forth above the upstairs bedrooms. At other times we hear a heavier clumping sound, as of a child pretending to walk like an adult. The running and walking footsteps are mischievous, kind of playful in feeling; I've never sensed that there was a frantic or angry edge to what was going on. These sounds have been heard at all times of day and night. They have been heard by everyone in my family and by three or four guests.

"We also hear a light tinkling sound like small bicycle bells. We first heard them during the summer, and thought the sound was caused by people riding by outside. When the ringing sounds continued into the dead of winter, we had to admit that they were coming from inside the building.

"We've heard doors opening and closing. All of the doors have latch fittings, and the *thunk-click* sound of a latch door is easy to identify. It's funny, because sometimes the door will actually open, and at other times you'll just hear the sound of it opening, but it will remain closed. That happens with the front door. It has a heavy wooden bar that runs across the back, and it sounds like no other door in the house. I'll be upstairs or in the kitchen, and at times I'll hear the door being opened and then closed. I must say it makes me nervous if I'm alone. I'll call out and then go to the entryway to look, and the door will still be firmly shut and locked as if nothing had happened.

"Once in a while all of the latches on the doors will start going up and down at once, making a rather maniacal rattling sound. When this happens during the day, it just seems curious and quite amazing, but when it happens at night I do get spooked. You can't help picturing unseen hands working away at the fittings. It's not a pleasant image.

"Another odd thing will happen when the house is in a particularly active phase. The windows have interior shutters, panels that fold back on themselves when open. There have been many times when my husband and I have been in the den talking or reading on a quiet night, and seen the shutters on each one of the windows being carefully opened and folded back. You will see the latch that fastens them being lifted, and both sets of panels slowly moving at the same time. My daughter was once in the living room with a friend from school, telling her about some of the odd goings-on in the house. Not surprisingly, her friend didn't believe her. Then they heard a scraping sound from across the room: one of the sets of shutters was being methodically opened. Her friend believed.

"My kids were teenagers when we first moved in, and I didn't tell them anything about the unexplained noises and sights that my husband and I had noticed in our new home. I didn't want them to start imagining things or feeling uncomfortable. This is important in light of the following story.

"It was our first summer in the house, and my son had a friend visiting. I believe his name was Kevin Flynn. It was a gorgeous, sunny day, and we were on our way to the beach. Everyone was outside in the car, and Kevin ran back in to get something he had forgotten in his bedroom. He galloped up the front stairs and went down the hall to his room. On the way out, he ran down the back way. When he reached the foot of the stairs, he saw three men standing by the kitchen table. They were dressed as if they had just stepped in out of a storm: they were wearing old-fashioned sou'westers—those rain hats with a broad brim—and long, black oilskins. Kevin said that he thought he remembered beards. They were there one moment, looking straight at him, as solid as could be, and then they vanished. It all happened in the blink of an eye.

"Kevin was, understandably, badly shaken. He sprinted back up the stairs, stuffed all of his things into his bag, and came out the front door looking very pale. He mumbled something about having to go, and made us drive him right to the airport. He flew home, never having given us a clue as to what had happened, and we really couldn't figure it out.

"Greg and I bumped into him on a plane a couple of years later. He came and sat with us, and it was then that he told us about the 'fishermen,' as he called them. He said that he just couldn't cope with the experience at the time; he was afraid to say anything for fear of being laughed at, and yet he was really too frightened to stay on in the house.

"My son Peter also saw three men. He was in his early twenties when this happened. He was headed down the hall to his room, which was dark even though the bathroom light was on behind him. He got to the doorway and found himself face-to-face with three figures. He said they weren't absolutely solid, but they were clearly men in bulky outdoor clothing. He said that they were also larger and somehow broader than they should have been. They were standing abreast, and they seemed to fill the room. He was scared and stayed absolutely still. He says that they moved rapidly toward him and right through where he was standing. It took him a long time to get over that; he turned all of the lights on every time he went upstairs at night, and slept with his bedside lamp on for the next two months.

"I could go on and on. There have been many separate incidents in the house over the years. My husband and I had an odd experience four or five years ago that I've always found intriguing and particularly strange.

"The house diagonally across the street from us is also old; it was built in the 1760s. I was handling a rental for that house and had heard from the owner, Elizabeth Chandless, that the house was haunted. She told me that some tenants from England had seen people going up and down the stairs and had heard constant rapping and knocking on the walls. She claimed that the house had been built for a woman by the name of Love Starbuck.

"I thought it was interesting, but I hadn't gotten around to mentioning it to my husband. We had a dinner party to go to that evening, and we didn't really have a chance to talk before going out.

"When we drove home after the party, my husband parked the car, which was a small convertible, in front of the Starbuck house. As he was putting up the roof, I walked across the street to our house and turned around at the front door. I thought about what Mrs. Chandless had told me, and as I looked at Love Starbuck's house I got a real chill—a kind of *uh-oh* sensation. I turned and hurried inside.

"Greg came in five minutes later looking absolutely white. He plopped down on the sofa and said, 'Shirley, I've just seen two ghosts.' Now, he is a rational, straightforward guy, and he's never been one to imagine things. He said he had put the car to bed for the night and crossed the street toward our house. As he approached, he saw two women standing in front of our door; they were talking in quiet voices and gesturing toward the Starbuck house behind him. One wore a Quaker bonnet, and they were in long skirts. He didn't think much of it, assuming they were coming home from a costume party of some kind. He glanced down as he stepped up on the curb, and when he raised his head, they had vanished. There was nowhere they could have gone in a split second—they had only been four or five yards away—and the street was empty. What can you say when something like that happens to you? I know he'll never forget it.

"One year around Christmas time, we had some friends over and the front doorbell rang. As I walked to the door I caught a glimpse, through the sidelights, of a young girl with long blond hair standing outside. We weren't expecting anyone else, but I said something like, 'Oh! That's funny,' and went to open the door. It was snowing outside, and there was no one in sight. Stranger still, there were no footprints on the sidewalk. One of my guests had also seen a young girl through the window, so I knew that I hadn't imagined it. And someone had rung the doorbell.

"Objects often get moved around the house. It's always a teasing sort of thing, but it can be trying. I have a nice gold lighter, and one night I had put it down on my bedside table. I turned to pick it up, and it was gone. I looked under the bed, around the table, even under the sheets. In fact, I practically pulled the bed apart looking for it. Finally, I sighed and went off to the bathroom. The room was empty for a moment, and when I returned, there was the lighter in the middle of my bed, right on top of the quilt.

"I'm quite aware of where I leave things, and our house is neat. Often I'll put a book down and just turn my head, only to find that the book has been moved to the floor or to another table. One day I lost a favorite silver serving piece. I went through everything in my kitchen looking for it. I finally found it stuffed in the back of a drawer where it certainly didn't belong. There's a naughty, now-you-see-it-now-you-don't quality to these happenings.

"I lost two diamond studs about six years ago. My cleaning lady just found one of them lying under a bed in our back bedroom. We painted and refinished the floor in there last year, so it couldn't possibly have been there all that time. I'm just hoping the other one will rematerialize also!

"When things get too wild in the house, when we have a period with a lot of shutter opening and door clicking and hidden objects, when it all gets to be a bit much, I just talk to the ghosts. I say exactly the same thing every time. Standing downstairs in the front room, I boom in my loudest, firmest voice, 'This is my house, and I'm taking very good care of it, and I want you to stop this right now!' And I've found that it works; everything will quiet down for a while.

"I wanted to talk to you outside of the house because I didn't want to get the place all stirred up. It's not that I'm afraid of all these goings-on, but I do believe that whatever or whoever causes these disturbances in the house is very much aware of what we do and say.

"Oh, Marianne!" A young woman had just passed our table, and Shirley asked me if I'd like to talk with her. She had spent a summer living in the Fergusons' house.

Marianne came over and sat down. "I can only stay for a minute, but I'd be happy to tell you about what happened. I can distinctly remember latches rattling, and I also remember being alone in the house one evening, downstairs, and seeing one of the sets of window shutters being opened. I wouldn't call myself a believer, but I *will* say that I saw things being done by people when there were no people there. That sounds ludicrous, but that's exactly what it was."

After Marianne had left, Shirley went on: "I truly love that house. I'm sure I'll own it for the rest of my life. We definitely share the house with an unseen contingent, and that isn't always pleasant, but the things that happen honestly don't scare me as much as they used to. That house is my home, and no home is perfect; some people put up with traffic noise, others with a bad heating system or a cramped kitchen. We put up with ghosts. I've heard of worse."

A Birdcage Table

"I should have been dead years ago, you know; I had cancer, and I was given two months to live after the operation. The women in my family have always been survivors. I'm just fine now, except that these legs don't work. During the winter I have to stay in town, but come summer I move to 'Sconset. Out there, I can sit in the front yard in my wheelchair and chat with everyone who goes by.

"I was born in 1911 in Irvington-on-the-Hudson. My parents summered on Nantucket from the time I was tiny. We used to travel on the ferry from New Bedford. The trip took about five and a half hours. My father would bring my sister and me up to meet the captain, which was thrilling, and then we'd go down and see the engine room, which I always found dreadfully boring. Father was fascinated by the giant wheels and chains and pipes. My sister and I fidgeted and perspired (it was broiling down there) and pulled on his hands to take us back to the stateroom.

"Once we arrived, we weren't allowed to swim for three days; we had to get 'acclimated' to the dangerous sea breezes before bathing. That was torture after waiting all winter to get to the beach. Once summer got under way, my sister and I went to the Jetties every morning. We had a bathhouse there for changing. Mornings, mind you; afternoons, the beach was reserved for the help. All the cooks and maids and housekeepers went down in the afternoon, and it was just understood that the families stayed home. It was quite a different world.

"My father bought our house on the north side of town when I was four years old. I'm trying to sell it now. It's a gorgeous eighteenth-century home, but needs a great deal of work, and no one in the family can afford to keep it. I've been warned by real estate agents not to say anything about ghosts, so I guess it's important that you disguise the location of the house and my name, silly as that sounds.

"When my sister and I were about ten and twelve, we were sitting around in the house with some friends one rainy day. My grandmother was visiting, and she told us about 'tipping tables,' which was a popular Victorian pastime. The idea was that several persons would gather around a table and rest their fingers lightly on the surface. They would address a question to a spirit, and the spirit would communicate by causing the table to rap with one leg on the floor.

"Of course we were fascinated. My sister and I wanted to try it. We sat down at a small round table in the parlor. It was a tilt-top birdcage tea table; it had three legs and had been made in the early nineteenth century by a cabinet-maker from Connecticut. The birdcage was a small open box on the underside of the table, purely decorative, with hand-turned spindles on all four sides.

"We rested our fingers on the surface of the table, and said something like, 'Is there a spirit in this house?' To our utter astonishment, the table started to move. It kind of rose up on one corner, and started to rap on the floor. My grandmother said, 'Quick—a pencil! We have to count!' The way it worked was that one rap stood for A, two for B, and so on. It took a long time to get a message down. The table rapped along for about ten minutes. When it stopped, we found we had a name. It was 'Alec Paddock.'

"From then on, my sister and I used to ask Alec questions, and he always answered. We could do it in front of any number of people. Word got around in the community that two little girls were 'tipping tables,' and to our delight, we became local celebrities.

"My father researched the house in the town records and found that a man by the name of Alec Paddock had indeed owned our home. Apparently, he had hanged himself in the keeping room.

"Alec seemed to be a friendly spirit and was very helpful. We asked him all kinds of pressing questions, such as, 'Is anybody going to invite us to the Yacht

Club dance?' and he always answered patiently. I don't remember him ever being wrong.

"Some of our communications were quite lengthy. He once spelled out something about being disturbed, and we asked him what the matter was. He said, 'I don't like the weeping stone.' No one had ever heard of such a term. It finally occurred to us that it might have to do with the structure of the house, and we asked a local mason if he had ever heard of a weeping stone. He said, 'Why, yes; there always used to be a damp spot somewhere next to the chimney in these old houses, a brick that drew and absorbed moisture.' Sure enough, we found the weeping stone in my bedroom, on one side of the fireplace. You could feel it through the plaster. It was quite wet, and still is. We hadn't even noticed it before, never having heard of such a thing.

"Alec told us at one point that there was treasure hidden in the attic. Of course my sister and I and our friends shrieked and scampered right up there, and one of us promptly fell through the ceiling of the second floor. My father was furious, and we had to give up on further attic investigations. I've always felt that there probably was money or jewelry hidden up there. If someone does extensive renovations on the house, I'm sure they'll turn up something valuable.

"Alec was outspoken. Some distant relatives stayed with us one summer, and one of them asked Alec a question while my sister and I were at the table. These people were rather difficult, and I don't remember being too fond of them. Alec spelled out, 'I don't like you. I wish you'd go home.'

"Alec was so communicative that people began coming to ask him questions about the stock market. I guess he was pretty good at giving them the answers they needed, because they kept coming back. It got to be a nuisance, in fact, and at one point my parents were bothered by a steady stream of visitors.

"One gentleman who called at the house was a researcher who specialized in exposing fraudulent mediums and 'fake' paranormal goings-on. He wanted to observe our table tipping. We didn't mind a bit. He said he was going to sit in the corner and think of a question to ask Alec. He would ask it silently, in his head. As proof, he wrote the question down and put it in his pocket.

"We sat down at the table. He sat in the corner. Pretty soon the table started to move. It rapped away, and the researcher counted the raps. When Alec was done, we had the message 'perelachaise.' My sister and I didn't know any French and wondered what this gobbledygook could mean. The researcher was dumbfounded. His question had been: 'Where is my good friend buried in France?' The answer was the Père Lachaise Cemetery.

"The same man did another experiment with us that was quite startling. He had us put our fingers lightly under the edge of the table and try to lift it while he was sitting on top. Amazingly, the table rose right up in the air. I can remember the feeling of lifting that table, researcher and all, as if it were a piece of paper.

"This man included us in a book that came out sometime in the thirties. My sister and I continued the rapping all through our teens, and it was only when we got married and went our separate ways that the table sat still.

"When my daughter and I cleared out the house last year, we sold a lot of the furniture. Rafael Osona, the auctioneer, got four thousand dollars for that little table. I never told him about Alec or the rapping. I'm sure the current owners would be surprised if they knew what that table used to do."

Silver Rings

"I know it's a man, but I don't know who he is or why he comes here. My husband and I built this house twenty years ago; we were the first to move into this wooded area. I've been on Nantucket since I was three, and my husband was born here. I'm a nurse, and I've worked night shifts at the hospital for nine years. My husband, who is no longer alive, was the manager of Nantucket Cablevision. Both of our families go back several generations on the island. Just a moment."

Carol Manville stood up and hurried out on the terrace. Her speech is shadowed by an easy, wide-brimmed laugh; one thinks of a shy person wearing a large hat. "You stay out of that water, Jackie! It's too cold to get soaking wet." Carol came back inside. "It's my grandson Jackie. He's a hot ticket. I'm watching him until my daughter Gussie gets off work. He's four years old and will get into just about anything you can think of.

"It's been so long that it's hard to remember how these visits began. As soon as we moved in, we began to hear things. Now, don't forget: We're talking about a brand-new house that was built in an area no one had lived in before. There've been no discoveries of old foundations, no handmade nails, broken china, arrowheads, bones. I've heard that this area was Starbuck land and was used for grazing sheep and cows many years ago.

"There are sliding-glass doors downstairs on the south side of the house. We were upstairs having supper one night, a few days after we had moved in, and we heard those doors open. Then we heard a man step inside and start walking around the first floor. He was whistling, the kind of soft, tuneless whistling a guy does while he's puttering in his shop. My husband called out and then went down. No one was there, and the sliding-glass door was closed.

"We heard this same sequence over and over and over. We kept the sliders locked, but we'd hear that door open—and it's an unmistakable sound, a scraping and a *shhhh* sound as the door is pushed open on its track—and then we'd hear footsteps. We sometimes heard the bedroom doors downstairs being opened and closed. The footsteps were not hurried, not scary, just a guy walking around as if he were busy doing his own thing. We only heard him when the kids and my husband and I were all upstairs. The sounds would go on for a couple of minutes, and let me tell you, two minutes is an eternity if you're listening to something strange. When we went downstairs, the sliders were always locked; this would have made it impossible, of course, for someone to open them from outside and walk in. If one of us (never me—I'm a coward) ran down there while the walking was going on, it would stop.

"I don't know why I'm putting all of this in the past tense. It happens during the day, it happens at night, it happens year-round, and it's gone on, as I said, for twenty years. There doesn't seem to be much pattern to it. Sometimes we'll hear this guy every day for three or four weeks and then there'll be a month or so with nothing. But he always comes back."

The front door slammed and Carol's daughter Gus came up the stairs. She gave her son a hug, poured herself a glass of soda, and plopped down in an armchair.

"Like Mom, I've heard him dozens of times over the years. And let me tell you, listening to that sound is no fun when you're in the house alone. I was once sitting on the sofa during the day, playing a game. My mom had been working all night, so she was asleep in her room. Suddenly I heard the knob to her bedroom door turning, and then the door flew open and whacked the wall with a bang. It didn't just open; it *crashed* open. I looked up, thinking, Uh-oh! We were making too much noise out here and she's really mad, but there was no Mom. I could see into her bedroom, and it looked dark. After a minute I tiptoed over and peeked in. She was sitting up in bed, her eyes very wide. The crash had startled her out of a deep sleep. No one visible had been anywhere near that door when it was opened."

Carol laughed and rubbed the back of her neck. "We've had some other weird things go on upstairs. The big stretch of wall over the stairwell used to be paneled, and we had an old map of the island and two black-and-white photographs hanging there. The photographs are of lighthouses, and the map is a navigational chart. My husband and I were sitting in the living room one night when all three pictures fell off the wall at once. The hooks were still in place, but the frames came down with a terrific crash. Nothing broke, amazingly, and we hung them up again.

"A couple of weeks later we were sitting in the living room with guests. With no warning, the same thing happened, this time with even greater violence. The hooks were bent, and the back of one frame was ripped right out. The map is really heavy, and it made an awful dent on the stair where it hit. I'll tell you, seeing those pictures come flying down was a real conversation-stopper. We all hollered. We never did hang them up again."

Carol left and returned carrying a two-by-three-foot chart mounted on a heavy wooden backing. It is labeled GEORGE ELDRIDGE'S CHART C: VINEYARD SOUND LIGHT SHIP TO CHATHAM. 1912.

"The photographs can be dated between 1900 and 1920. Now look at this print: the hook tore clean through the backing. That would take a very strong arm, but of course it wasn't an arm because all three were yanked down simultaneously.

"We did tell the people who were visiting us that night about some of the other bizarre things that've gone on, but if someone's in the house and the whistling or footsteps start up, I won't say anything if they don't ask. It's a touchy subject, and you don't want to sound like a drinker or a nut case."

Gus laughed. "It's pretty hard to believe unless you're right there. When I was in high school, most of my friends heard the ghost at some point when they were visiting. But I never brought up the subject unless something just happened."

Jackie came in and climbed up on Gus's lap. She pulled some chips of bark off his sweater. "Oh! I almost forgot the rings," she said. "We had several weeks when silver rings kept showing up. I was still living at home; I must have been sixteen or seventeen. Mom doesn't wear rings, and I never have either; I've worked in restaurant kitchens for years, and they just get in your way.

"Mom found a little silver ring sitting on the dining room table one day. Assuming it was something I had bought, she put it up on the mantel. A few days later, she found two more rings in the cabinet where we keep glasses. She found another on the kitchen counter. One day she asked me if I could please put my rings away. I said, 'What rings?' I'd never seen them before.

"There was no one staying here who could have left jewelry around, I didn't have a boyfriend at that time, and we asked friends and family who had been at the house if they had any idea where the rings had come from. It's a real mystery. Those rings turned up out of nowhere, and they were in obvious places, places where you couldn't miss them.

"They weren't old rings and they didn't look like particularly expensive ones, but they were sterling. I still have them all in my jewelry box. One had a little knot in it. One had a lot of flattened sides; I think it was octagonal. One had a little wave in it, and one had a heart. And they fitted me."

Carol smiled. "Maybe there was some connection between Gus not wearing those rings and the pictures crashing down. I hadn't thought of that one before. I honestly can't remember which happened first, but that would make sense: he got mad!"

Carol went on. "I did see him. That's how we know it's a man. I was alone in the house in the middle of the afternoon, washing vegetables at the sink and talking on the phone. I suddenly felt something behind me, and I turned around. It was someone in his fifties, I'd say, and I could see through him. His body was misty; it was translucent. He was only ten to twelve feet away, facing me, standing very still just inside the terrace door. I stood by the sink, my mouth probably hanging open, and watched him just fade into nothing. I suppose I only saw him clearly for a second or two. He was heavyset and was wearing what looked like work clothing; I can remember a plain, button-down shirt. I didn't get the impression that his outfit was old-fashioned. And, strangely enough, I didn't feel afraid of him—he didn't seem like a bad presence—but I'll tell you, I *was* shaken up. I can remember my girlfriend on the other end of the phone saying, 'Carol? Hello? Are you there?' and me saying, 'Uh, there's someone here in the kitchen with me . . .'

"This presence in our home is just something we've always lived with. The kids became used to it, and we've had to accept the whistling and the steps and all as something that is part of our lives. My husband and I were careful not to frighten the kids. We always tried to sound very ho-hum about these visits.

"I've had one other experience with ghosts on the island. When our kids were very young, we lived in a house on the northwest edge of the Old North Burial Ground. It was a protected spot with short grass and lots of room to run, so I used to let the kids squeeze through the hedge and play in there. They never hurt anything.

"One night something really awful happened in that house. I was in the living room, straightening up at the end of the day, and I suddenly felt frightened. I turned around, and there was a figure in black, a tall figure in a robe. It sounds like a cheap movie, but that is what I saw. He had a soft covering, a hood of some sort, draped over his head. The air in the room went ice cold, deathly cold, and I was so stunned, so overwhelmed, that I couldn't seem to react in any way. My feet kind of melted into the floor. One of my sons was playing in the corner, and he screamed. He could obviously see and feel what I was seeing and feeling. The figure was cloudy, not as solid as a living person, but it was plenty real. And it felt so bad, so threatening. Then, just as suddenly as it had turned up, it was gone, and the room felt normal and the temperature warm again. I rushed over to my son and grabbed him. I felt as though I had just seen Death himself.

"Gus also had a nasty experience in that house. She woke up one night shortly after that, yelling like a wild thing, saying that she saw a man. Do you remember that, Gus?"

"Sure I remember. I opened my eyes and saw a broad-shouldered guy in black clothes standing in the corner of my room. And then, by the time Mom came in, he was gone; he vanished into thin air. But it wasn't a dream or a shadow. I was awake, and he was *there*. He scared the heck out of me. I had nightmares about that figure for years."

Carol shifted on the sofa, as if suddenly tired. She continued, "No one in our family ever saw the man again, but I did have a weird experience with two young kids I used to take care of while we were in that house. The kids were about four and five, and they liked to play in the part of the cemetery that bordered our property. They told me that they met a friend there called Mary Abby and that she was littler than they were. They said she was looking for her father. I never saw anyone out there with them, and I assumed the girl was an imaginary character they had dreamed up.

"One day, Gus, who was in third grade, was outside playing with the kids. A corner of the graveyard, one that bordered the woods near our house, had been overgrown with at least five feet of brambles and weeds for as long as we could remember. Gus noticed that someone from the town had finally gotten in there and cleared out the undergrowth. She was thrilled, of course, to have this corner all cleaned up, and she took the kids right over to look at the stones that had been uncovered.

"One of the marble headstones, a little one, said 'Mary Abby Swain.' The child had died on May 30, 1837, when she was two and a half years old."

A Lady in Black

The house was standing by 1733. The first floor is firmly anchored by a massive wisteria vine, which some sixty years ago was coaxed from the front wall of the building, where it was commandeering windows and trim, to a freestanding trellis. One can see why it wasn't simply cut back. In winter the wisteria has a heavy, arthritic aspect, but come spring it turns, in a matter of days, into a frivolous cloud of lavender and pale green.

Dr. and Mrs. Franklin Addison bought the property in 1939, and left it to their daughter and her husband, Laura and Jim Fargo, in 1964. The Fargos lived in Illinois for twenty-seven years and retired to Nantucket in 1980.

The front entryway is just large enough to allow the door to swing all the way open. Stepping inside, one comes face-to-face with a steep spiral staircase; each tread, a marvel of knots and fissures and hollows, tells its own story of human use. A thick rope hangs down the inside of the stairwell from the second story.

The ceilings on the first floor are irregular in height and unusually low; they range from six feet two inches in the dining room and east parlor to about seven feet in the keeping room. The bedrooms, upstairs, have higher ceilings; perhaps conservation of heat was not as important (or was quite futile) on the second floor. As with any eighteenth-century home, there seem to be no right angles and no absolutely flat surfaces. Plastered walls and ceilings stretch, rippling, between corner posts and massive overhead beams, and each fireplace has its own set of dimensions. In comparison, the regularity of a modern house looks all too predictable.

"Her name is Flora Perreira and she lives out near Five Corners. She's going to be ninety next August. She's as sharp as can be and still working; she takes in ironing and does a little mending for people. Flora is the only one, as far as I know, who has ever seen our so-called lady in black."

Laura Fargo has salt-and-pepper hair and a cautious smile. There is something sparrowlike about her speech; she hops quickly from one sentence to the next, pausing briefly to assess her whereabouts. She went on: "Flora worked for my parents during the forties. I know she saw an apparition in the house several times, but she never went into great detail about her experiences. Although she loves to chat, she always managed to change the subject when someone brought it up. She may have been scared of the ghost; she may have felt it just shouldn't be talked about; she may have been superstitious—I don't know. I still visit her regularly, but I don't think I've mentioned the ghost in eighteen years.

"I have had only one truly unpleasant experience in this house, and it's really nothing next to Flora's stories. One night about ten years ago, I was here all by myself and woke up sometime after midnight. Our bedroom is right over the old section of the living room. I found myself sitting bolt upright, looking at a corner of the room to the left of the fireplace. I couldn't see anything, but I felt as though something or someone was really after me. It's hard to describe. I was petrified. I was here alone, and I had no choice: I could either run into the street in my nightgown or face this thing. I tried to confront it mentally, to let it know that I wasn't scared. It did gradually go away. Nothing like that has ever happened again.

"We have seen latch doors opening in the house. I was once tidying around upstairs in our bedroom and saw the latch lift on our bathroom door. I thought my husband was coming out, but when he didn't appear after several minutes, I called out to him and then opened the door. No one was there. Our kitchen door also occasionally opens on its own.

"I used to be really scared of this house, I guess because of Flora's experiences, and I didn't want to be. When we moved here year-round, I decided to try to settle this business once and for all. I walked into the middle of the living room and said in a firm voice, 'You'd be much happier outside, away from here. It's time for you to leave.' And do you know, I really think it worked. At any rate, I'm no longer scared to go into the living room at night (yes, I used to be!) and I don't feel like there's anything menacing lingering in the house.

"Now, it really would be something if Flora would tell you what happened herself. I doubt she will, because she always seemed to hate talking about the ghost, but I'll ask. I'm going over to see her on Tuesday.

"Fred Sargeant keeps an eye on the house when we're away. You might also want to talk to him. Although we never mentioned anything about ghosts to Fred, he did tell us several years ago that he felt there was a presence here."

Fred Sargeant:

"I take care of the Fargos' house when they're not here. I've been doing it for four years now. When I first started, I had a golden retriever puppy, and I used to take the dog with me. He would follow me in the side door of the house to the mud room and stop dead at the door to the kitchen. There was nothing I could do to get him to go any farther. He just wouldn't do it. He would look miserable, lie down, try to sneak back out the door. He's a dog who would ordinarily bounce right into any house and start dashing all over. I was never able to get him to even cross the kitchen with me.

"Another thing I didn't like much was that the latch door between the kitchen and the hall was always open when I went in. When I left, I always shut that door firmly. A latch with a good fitting doesn't just pop open by itself."

Flora Perreira:

"We just didn't agree about the window shades. That was the only real trouble I had with her. It was just plain aggravating, it was, because I'd have to keep running back into the living room from the kitchen and peeping at the shades to see if they was still the way I'd left them. I was the only maid working for Mrs. Addison, you see, and that's a pretty big house. I took care of all the cooking, served the meals, and did the cleaning. I did love the Addisons and we had a very good relationship, don't get me wrong, but there was a lot to be done every day, and I must say I got *furious* about what she did to those window shades.

"I worked for Dr. and Mrs. Addison from '41 to '48. Oh yes, I surely do remember the first time I saw her. I don't mind talking about it now, but at the time it happened it shook me up pretty bad. It was shortly after I came to work at the house. I walked into the living room from the north side and there she was, standing big as life by the front door. That first time I saw her I couldn't believe it. I'd never seen a spirit before. She didn't look like a living person; I'd say she was more of a shadow or an image. She looked the way people do if you see them through a curtain, you know? You could see her pretty clear, but you couldn't make out her expression or, say, the buttons on her dress. And she was really small. I'm five-foot-two, and she was much shorter than I am. It seemed like she was only about four feet high and as wide as she was tall. She was what you might call overweight. She had one of those little caps on with a ruffle around the face, like they used to wear, and long black skirts that went right down to the ground. I never saw her move, but then I didn't stand around visiting, either. I'd hustle right on out of the room whenever I saw her, and that first time, I do believe I ran. Over the years I got kind of used to her, I guess you'd say, but I didn't go trying to interfere or make friends.

"As I said, we had this running battle about the window shades. See, the only place I ever saw her was in the living room. It's a big room, large for such an old house, and it has lots of windows in it, maybe ten or twelve. The Addisons used to have coffee in the living room every evening. While they were finishing dinner I'd go in and pull each one of the shades down. I'd leave the room, and a few minutes later the shades would be up again. And if it happened in the morning, it would work the other way around. I'd go in to pull the shades up and then leave to set the breakfast table; I'd peep back in the living room, and darn if those shades weren't down again! There's a big wisteria

146

vine on the front of the house, and during the summertime it gets awful dark in the living room because of all those leaves, so those shades need to be *all* the way up.

"If I pulled the shades down, she'd pull them up; if I pulled them up, she'd pull them down. If I pulled them halfway she'd pull them all the way, and so on. And there was nothing wrong with the shades; sometimes one of the family would fix them and they'd stay right where they were put. I guess the lady and I just didn't agree about things. It wasn't bad, but as I said before, it was just plain aggravating, especially when I had a lot of things to do.

"I saw her any number of times over the years; sometimes I'd see her two or three times a week. She was usually near the fireplace, which is one of those real big old hearths. She was always slightly bent over, looking in at the andirons. I used to wonder if she'd buried something under a brick, but I suppose she'd just spent a lot of time cooking there and thought she was still checking the soup. Who knows?

"The Addisons had two love seats in the living room, one facing out toward the back garden, which was a peaceful view, and the other facing the street. I'd be tidying around the house, and I'd come into the living room and find the love seats turned around: one would be facing the fireplace, and one would be looking out over the side lawn. That happened many times. She also used to move that tall standing lamp by the front door right out into the room, and it was a mighty heavy piece of iron. I had to struggle to move it myself. Oh, she had definite ideas about how she wanted the living room. The odd thing was that those weren't her belongings, you know; the shades, the love seats, and the lamp were all things that Mrs. Addison had brought to the house.

"If the weather was bad in the evening, I'd sometimes stay over in the maid's room back near the kitchen. Well, I'd go in and turn on the light and pull the shades—there were lots of big bushes out back—and then I'd leave to wash the dinner dishes. When I'd come back in, the shades would be up. No, we just plain didn't agree on how things should be.

"Dr. and Mrs. Addison went to Florida in the winter, and she'd write and tell me when they were coming back to Nantucket. I'd make the beds up maybe two days before they arrived, because the fog gets in under those sheets and they get awful clammy and damp if you leave them too long. Well, no sooner would I do the beds in Dr. and Mrs. Addison's room and leave to make up the guest bedroom or Miss Laura's room, than the sheets would be pulled right off. I'd go back into the room, and there they'd be in a heap on the floor, those nice clean sheets that I'd just washed and ironed. That happened sometimes even when the Addisons were in the house. I'd get so mad. I once said, out loud, 'Don't you *dare* touch those sheets!' That seemed to help for a few weeks.

"I remember one evening when the Addisons had gone into the living room after dinner and were sitting in the love seats, reading. Mrs. Addison read all the time; she always had a book in her hands, indoors or out. Well, I came in carrying a tray with coffee, and as I went over the threshold into the living room I was looking down, because I've always been clumsy with my feet. When I looked up, with the tray in my hands, I near died. There she was, leaning over Mrs. Addison's shoulder, right up close to the side of her head. It's one thing to see a spirit across a room and another to see one a few inches away from a living person. My first thought was that the lady was going to try to hurt Mrs. Addison, she was so near, but Mrs. Addison never even knew the lady was there. I guess that the spirit was just trying to see what Mrs. Addison was reading.

"Dr. Addison belonged to something called the Winter Club, and they'd get together at each other's houses once in a while and talk about heaven knows what and have something to eat and drink. Well, one time when the Winter Club was coming, I made all the sandwiches early and put them out on the kitchen table. I had them stacked one on top of the other so they wouldn't dry out, and I had covered them with a napkin. I left the room for a bit, and when I came back the sandwiches were spread all over the platter and it looked like some were missing. I asked Mrs. Addison if she had taken some of them, and she said, 'Oh, no, Flora. You know I'd never interfere with how you do things in the kitchen.' And she never did. I suppose the lady just didn't like the way I had the sandwiches arranged. I think she really felt, you know, that she still owned the house.

"I left in '48, but I kept in touch with the Addisons, and when Mrs. Addison died in 1970, her daughter, Mrs. Fargo, called me on the phone. She told me she and her son were coming to the island and asked if I could go in and freshen things up a bit before they arrived. Of course I was happy to. Well, would you believe it—I walked into that living room and there she was. She looked just the same. She was still in black, with that little cap on, standing very still in the corner of the room. I'd never been overly fond of her, but I found myself thinking, 'Oh, that poor thing! Alone all these years!' I turned my back on her and went around pulling up the shades. Sure enough, before I had even left the room, the shades were pulled right back down, one by one. Next I went to take the sheets off all the paintings. I got to one painting, a portrait of a gentleman in Mrs. Fargo's family, and as I reached up to take down the sheet, a low voice behind me said clearly, 'Don't.' There was just that one word. That was the first time I had heard her speak, and I'll tell you, I didn't touch that sheet. I'm afraid it was still on the painting when Mrs. Fargo arrived.

"As I said before, I left in '48; Mrs. Addison needed a nursemaid for her grandchildren and couldn't afford to keep me on too. Well, I got to be friends with the woman she hired. Her name was Connie Newman. Connie always felt that the lady in black didn't like her at all.

"A funny thing used to happen to Connie in the living room. She would go out the back door to the porch on the northwest side, you know, and no sooner was she outside than that big old door would slam behind her and lock. Now, in order to lock it, you have to place a long board across the inside of the door and fasten it with a wooden peg. It was only when Connie dragged a really heavy armchair in front of the door to prop it open that it wouldn't slam to and lock her out.

"Connie used to visit me sometimes on her day off, and she'd tell me what was happening in the household and what the lady in black was up to. She'd say to me, 'Flora, why don't you think she likes me?' She was a sweet person, much sweeter by nature than I am, and everybody liked her. She was lame, and really round and short. I'd say, 'Well, Connie, maybe she don't like you because you're fat like she was.' Connie would laugh and laugh.

"I never saw the lady upstairs, but Connie did many times. She used to see her standing quietly in the master bedroom above the living room. At one point Connie had the baby's bassinet up there. Some days she'd be outside working when she'd hear the baby start fussing. Well, of course she'd hurry on up, which took her a few minutes, being lame and all. By the time she got upstairs, the baby would often be happily waving her hands and making sounds the way she did when someone was entertaining her. Connie would frown, even if she couldn't see the lady, and snatch the baby up and hurry downstairs. But I said, 'Why Connie, what'd you do that for? They were perfectly happy!'

"Connie said that she had a lot of trouble, more trouble than I really had, with things being moved and rearranged in the living room. One of the things I remember her telling me about concerned a beautiful glass and satin screen, the kind of standing screen you put up behind a chair to stop drafts. It had four sections, and it was really heavy. Connie said she used to find it carefully moved across the room and folded up against one of the love seats. That lady in black must've been awful strong.

"Here's something funny. Connie said she used to wash out her underwear and hang it up to dry in the bathroom next to the maid's room. Well, the next time she'd go back in there, the underwear would all be back in the tub soaking, ready for another washing. I told Connie that maybe the lady thought she used too much soap and needed to rinse things out better. Oh, that lady was particular, she was."

Heart

"I was sixteen years old when we moved. I went around the entire house, from room to room, saying good-bye to it. My dream is to buy that house back and completely restore it, return it to its original state.

"Growing up in a haunted house was, for me, a fact of life: it wasn't bad and it wasn't good. It just was. The house had a distinct will, or perhaps I should say a set of moods, that existed regardless of whatever we did inside it. I was aware of that from the time I was very young."

Trisha Murphy, the bookkeeper for the Nantucket Historical Association, was seated in a square of January sunshine in her apartment at the Beachside Motel. She was caretaking the complex for the winter. Her back was turned to the sliding-glass doors, and the white light pouring in caught in her hair, forming a plump, shimmery halo.

Trisha looked at her mother, Ann, who was sitting on the sofa: "Mom, your feelings about the house weren't as positive as mine, were they? I mean, you weren't as attached to it."

"Oh, I wouldn't say that. We owned the house for twenty years. That's a long time. I guess you could say I was leery of that building. It was home, but it wasn't always mine. I mean, I wasn't always in control of the place."

Mrs. Murphy, very neat in a blue permapress pants suit, crossed her arms. She continued, "My husband, Paul, and I came to the island twenty-eight years ago, and we wanted to stay. We had a young family, and thought that if we owned a guesthouse I could take care of the rentals and still be home with the kids.

"The house is enormous, and it had been cut up into five apartments by the previous owner. It was too expensive for us to heat the whole building during the winter, so we rented the apartments all summer and then closed them down once the cold set in.

"The house is, I understand, one of the few Victorian gems on the island. It was built by Charles H. Robinson, who also built the great Sea Cliff Inn just down the road. It was the era of grand hotels, you know, of buildings that were the equivalent of palaces by the sea. They went in for gorgeous paneling and woodwork, stained-glass windows, crystal, Oriental rugs. Our house was built between 1881 and 1890 for a banker by the name of R. Gardner Chase. Something went wrong, for he declared bankruptcy in 1891.

"The house went from R. Gardner Chase's creditors to Colonel and Mrs. John W. Summerhayes. Martha Summerhayes, who was then a widow, sold the house in 1913 to Helen E. MacKay. The house passed to the MacKay children and grandchildren and then was bought by the Lennons in 1957. Evelyn Lennon was a hairdresser who used to go to the house to 'do the old Mrs. MacKay's hair.' She bought the place for the antiques, or so she told me when we moved in. I guess she sold a lot of the valuable belongings in there, because the house was pretty much stripped of furnishings when we bought it. Paul and I owned the house from 1961 to 1981.

"It's a crazy building; I don't think any two windows in the entire place are the same size, and the house is almost boastful about its irregularities. I guess that was the idea. Every room is different from every other. As Trisha said, the house has a strong character of its own.

"When we were comparing notes recently about our memories of the place, Trisha and I realized that, while we were living in it, we hardly ever discussed the odd things that went on in the house. To be truthful, I think I was afraid to. I was willing to admit to myself that there were spirits in the building, but I thought that if I recognized them, talked about them, it would either make them angry or encourage more funny stuff. All of us knew about the stranger aspects of our home, but, as if we had agreed on it, we didn't verbalize our fears. It wasn't until Trisha and I were talking the other day that she and I realized how similar our feelings about specific areas of the house were."

"Most of the bad experiences were connected with the two stairwells," Trisha added. "As Mom said, and I think this may be relevant, the house was pretty much untouched, architecturally, when we lived there. All the original interior details—moldings, fireplaces, stairwells—were still there, looking just as they had in 1890.

"I had the run of the house during the winter. I can remember one Christmas when I was nine or ten, and I had taken some wrapping paper and presents up to the third-floor landing. I had everything spread out on the floor and was folding and taping away when I was struck by a horrendous feeling.

"I should explain that there was a back stairwell for servants that ran from the cellar to the third floor, opening onto the main stairwell landings at each level. The intent was for maids and housekeepers to have a way to carry food and laundry through the house without using the main staircase. There was nothing visually spooky about those back stairs; they were well lit by exterior windows and were in good condition.

"I was kneeling, facing the closed door to the back stairwell. The door was probably locked; we never used those stairs. Suddenly I knew that there was something terribly evil on the other side of that door. I don't mean to sound overly dramatic, but evil is the only word for it. It was as if something deadly, something utterly dark, was standing on the other side of the door. Dropping everything, I tore down the front stairs, burst into our apartment, and slammed the door."

"Oddly enough," Ann picked up, "I had a very bad feeling about that third-floor landing also. At times I would walk by and feel as though something nasty, something really bad, was inches away from me. I can remember one time when I was alone in the house and was walking downstairs from the top floor. I had hurried by the third-floor landing, having gotten that oh-no feeling, and was by the second-floor landing when I heard footsteps coming down the stairs, *bam-bam-bam-bam*, very businesslike, from above. I didn't look up. I didn't look anywhere. I just ran. That's no fun, being bullied in your own house.

"The cellar stairs were also a bad area. The cellar had a dirt floor, and nothing in it had been changed from the day the house was built. We kept the clothes dryer down there. There were times when I'd be walking up those cellar stairs carrying a load of laundry and I'd know there was someone behind me. It was a dreadful, spine-chilling feeling; I just had to hustle up the stairs as fast as I could and slam the door. I was a grown woman, and I knew the sensation couldn't hurt me, but there was no way I could face that instinctive fear. I was being chased up the stairs by something invisible. I just had to run."

"Mom's not exaggerating," Trisha continued. "I remember having that same sense: I'd be walking up those stairs, and on some days, wow! There it would be behind you, something really bad. I can remember locking that door and leaning against it. There was a round hole that you could stick your finger in to pull the door open, and I remember looking at that hole and expecting to see a finger poking through to find me."

"Oh, Trisha! That's dreadful. And I didn't know, all the time we were living there, that Trisha had these terrifying moments too. Part of it, I'm sure, is that whatever was in the house only bothered us individually. It never happened to two of us at the same time. When something strange like that happens to you and you're by yourself, you're much less likely to talk about it."

"Mom and I had many more of those unpleasant experiences than my father or older sister and brother had," added Trisha. "It may have been because we simply spent more time in the house. Mom cleaned all the apartments regularly, and when I was little and my brother and sister were in school, I spent hours just playing by myself.

"I always knew, as Mom did too, that I was safe if I could get behind a closed door. It doesn't make sense, because I suppose that whatever was bothering us could get through a door easily, but we reacted the same way: if one of us had a frightening experience, we'd run into a nearby room and shut the door. It seemed to work. I can remember thinking to myself, 'Get into a room! *Shut the door!* Shut the door, and you'll be okay!'

"The main stairwell was very open, very formal, and when you were standing on it, you felt terribly exposed. It was almost as if you were being watched. I think we all felt it. My dad was on the third floor one day, and the house was empty. I believe he was doing some repair work. He heard someone walking all the way up the main stairwell from the ground floor, right up to the door of the room he was working in. He thought one of us had gotten home, and he called out. No one responded. He opened the door and looked around. It hadn't been one of us. He was pretty rattled by that one.

"Yes," Ann picked up. "I remember him saying to me, 'What the heck is going on here?' All we could do was laugh it off; we couldn't explain it and we couldn't control it. As for the other things that went on upstairs, I had one closet door on the third floor that would open by itself, but only when *I* cleaned the room. I could close it firmly and latch it, and then turn around and start vacuuming again. When I looked back the door would be wide open. Whenever that happened, when I got one of those creepy someone's-in-the-room-with-me feelings, I'd just leave. I didn't fight it.

"I was once in one of the second-floor bedrooms and heard a steady rapping on the walls that started in the front entryway and rose clear up the stairwell, around and around, right up to the door of the room I was in. It was a loud, strong knock, just like the knock on a door, except it went on and on. I thought it might be my husband or son trying to play tricks on me, and I called out. No one answered, and it turns out that they weren't even in the house. Now that was scary, worse than hearing footsteps, I think, because it sounded like a form of communication. No way was I going to develop a relationship with spirits in my house. Trisha, you once heard knocking too, didn't you?"

"Yes. I was about ten, and I heard it coming all the way up the back stairwell to the top floor. It wasn't wood expanding and contracting, it was a steady, hard rapping that you could hear approaching. I ran and shut myself in one of the rooms until I felt it was safe to come out.

"I had a persistent image connected with that third-floor landing," Trisha continued. "It was something I could see out of the corner of my eye, it would just kind of flit by, and then when I looked right at the spot where I'd seen movement, it would be gone. The image was of a stocky woman dressed all in black. She had floor-length clothing and a black veil over her head. One moment she was there, and the next she wasn't; it was just the briefest sensation.

"Mom had a very real run-in with a figure downstairs—didn't you?"

"I did." Ann paused to light a cigarette. "I went into our oldest daughter's room to check on her one night. Our apartment was located to the left of the front door, as you entered the building; it had once been the kitchen area and pantry, and I never had any bad feelings in there.

"As I said, for some reason I went to check on my oldest daughter, who was then eleven years old. I saw a form, clearly human and the size of an adult, bending over the foot of her bed. It was almost transparent, and had a long, pale gown on. I must have made a noise, and it straightened up and backed away from me. After a couple of steps it evaporated into thin air.

"I know that what I saw wasn't bad, because it didn't frighten me. Some of the other things in the house were terrifying, but this figure just wasn't scary. It didn't feel scary. When my daughter was thirteen, the same thing happened all over again. The figure was standing in the same position, it reacted in the same way, and it disappeared. My daughter never even woke up or stirred, and I didn't tell her about these visits until after we'd sold the house.

"I'm convinced there was more than one spirit in that building. The difference between the form bending over my daughter's bed and the feeling around the stairwell was like day and night. That dark feeling was so threatening, so filled with poison and hatred, that Trisha and I wondered, in trying to figure it out, if someone was once pushed down the back stairs. Something very violent must have happened.

"I'm sure of it. Mom," Trisha interjected. "Some ghastly thing must have taken place in that house. And yet I really loved the place and felt generally very safe there. It was as if there were certain warped or diseased feelings trapped in the building, but the soul of the place, its essence, was kindly. And I meant what I said about wanting to own the house again; I would love to take care of it. We never heard anything about ghosts from the man who bought it from us, but then I think he just about gutted it. He got rid of most of the original trim and interior woodwork, and perhaps in the process he did the building a service. Who knows? He may have freed whatever was imprisoned inside those walls."

The following letter was received from Trisha Murphy six weeks after the interview took place:

Dear Blue,

We spoke in March in regard to the ghosts at our former residence. I was recently discussing the subject of our talk with my brother, and he brought up something both my mother and I had forgotten. Objects sitting on the mantel of a room that was originally the library used to tick. The object that would tick most often was a ceramic heart. This heart had been given to us by a relative. It was not an original item in the house. The heart could not have been rocking from the disturbance of passing cars, because it had a felt covering on the bottom.

I remember hearing the sound and following it to the heart on more than one occasion. My brother, who at one point slept in that room, said that if he touched the heart something else on the mantel would begin to tick. My brother said he also shared my mother's and my feelings about something chasing him up the cellar stairs. It's strange, but even to this day when we discuss it, we still get that terrifying feeling we felt when strange things happened, as if we were reliving it.

Just thought you might be interested.

A Nocturnal Twirl

"As long as I have my cup of tea after work, I'm fine; until then, I'm a bear. Anita and I get home a little after five and go right in and put the kettle on. This is English tea. We make it good and strong. Here you are—can't have it without milk and sugar.

"I work for the Nantucket Police Department, and Anita's a librarian at the Atheneum. Anita's a Stackpole, you know. She's a twelfth-generation Nantucketer." Ed Dougan leaned forward, forming a generous triangle of forearms, hands, and mug on the kitchen table. Steam rose from the apex.

Anita smiled. "Yes, I'm part Gardner, part Swain, part Coffin, part Starbuck, part Folger. The genealogical charts are wild when you get back that far; a husband and wife in the nineteenth century might have been related to each other four or five times over. The family lines crossed and recrossed each other in the dizziest way.

"I've often wondered how many twelfth- and thirteenth-generation Nantucketers are left on the island; that is, people who are descended from the original nine settlers. I guess we're what you'd call an endangered species.

"Being a native gives one definite coloration; you carry with you a sense of belonging, a clearly defined feeling of origin. Of course, the flip side of the coin is that islanders are afraid to live anywhere else, which isn't right. I feel bad for the young ones who've only been as far as Hyannis and never experienced any other kind of life. Ed and I have lived all over. He was in the Air Force for twenty-two years, and when he retired, at the age of forty-one, we moved to Panama for fourteen years. We'd stay down there during the winter and come back to Nantucket to work and see the family every summer."

"Yup. I was in the military for a long time and then I became a beach bum. It was great. We had a scuba diving business in Panama," Ed went on. "You talk about a tropical paradise. We spent quite a bit of time in the little islands that sit off the coast. There are three hundred between Colon and Columbia. Some are only inhabited by the Cuna Indians, and some are absolutely deserted.

"We got very close to the Indians. When we lived on San Bias, the local chieftain had forbidden his tribe to use any diving equipment because two young men had gotten the bends and died while diving. So that's where Anita and I came in: The chieftain was happy to have somebody else take over what looked to him like an insane activity.

"I'll never forget the day a boatload of tourists landed from one of the big ships, and a man in the launch pointed at me and yelled, 'Hey! Hey!' I thought at first that he'd gone berserk. 'I know you!' he said. 'You're the miller on Nantucket! You're the goddamn miller!'

"And so I was. I ran the mill from 1977 to 1980. Anita worked with me for two of those years. And that's where we ran into a little ghost activity.

"Now, you know that the mill was built in 1746. It was designed and put together by Nathan Wilbur, a Nantucket seaman who had been to Holland and seen what wind power was really capable of. He had a vision, and he was a master craftsman. The result was a building that is now one of the most extraordinary eighteenth-century mills still operating in the United States.

"The mill is a tapered octagonal structure that rises fifty feet from the ground. All the joints were tightly dovetailed, and I don't believe there's a right angle to be seen anywhere in that building. Wilbur used hickory pins instead of nails to secure the framework; a hole had to be cut for each pin before it was driven into place. He worked with white oak beams and deck planking salvaged from shipwrecks.

"The millstones Wilbur used were granite and weigh about two thousand pounds each, which is relatively light for a grinding stone. His was the first mill in New England in which the stones were set on the second story.

"The challenge for Nathan Wilbur must have been in putting the project together, because he sold the mill the following year to Eliakim Swain and John Hay. They sold it in 1750 to Timothy Swain.

"Timothy Swain was an eccentric man. He was either a devoted miller or a poor sleeper, for when the winds were favorable he would run the mill at night. People would say that Swain was out doing a 'nocturnal twirl.' One morning the town woke up to find the mill grinding away at dawn and Timothy Swain dead inside. He had died, apparently, of natural causes.

"Charles Swain ran the mill for many years after Timothy, and Charles's grandson Nathan Swain owned it until 1828. It must have been in bad shape, because in that year Jared Gardner, who lived next door, bought the mill for twenty dollars 'for firewood.' Gardner probably never had any intention of chopping it up; after purchasing it, he repaired the mill and operated it himself until 1855. George Enos bought it and ran it until 1864, when it went to Captain John Murray, and then to a Portuguese man by the name of John Francis Sylvia.

"The mill ran sporadically during the 1870s and then sat silent until 1897, when it was sold at auction. Everyone assumed it would be torn down. It was bought by Miss Caroline French, a summer person, who turned around and gave it to the Nantucket Historical Association. And they've taken good care of it.

"Running the mill is a tricky thing, and it's exhausting work if you do it right. I had a feel for it, which some millers never do. I don't know quite how to explain it. You get in tune with the mill. It's almost like sailing a boat. You feel the vibration of the works, you listen to the sounds; you get to know the creaks and rattles and moans of the teeth, the millstones, the shaker box, the building itself, and you can gauge wind velocity and just how fast the mill is running.

"The mill itself can be a very dangerous mechanism, and you have to stay on top of it. You need to be continually adjusting the beam, which in turn raises or lowers the grinding stone a thousandth of an inch to compensate for a wind shift. I'm very proud of the fact that I'm the only miller, as far as I know, who has never broken one of the hickory teeth on the flywheel. No sir, I've never broken a single tooth, and I know that on several occasions as many as thirty or forty teeth have been stripped when the mill got away.

"When the mill is running on an even keel, you can tie off the beam, kind of like cleating the tiller. When doing that, I discovered something very odd: as soon as I got to the other side of the room, directly across from that beam, the mill would suddenly pick up speed and I'd have to go running back. It seemed that I could *make* this happen. The mill would be running in a good steady wind, without needing any adjustment, and I'd walk exactly to that halfway point by the stairs, and the mill would take over. It happened literally hundreds and hundreds of times. Anita and I used to laugh about it. I could do it in front of a crowd of people. I'd show them where I was going to walk and what was going to happen when I got over there, and it always happened just as I'd predicted.

"It was almost as if there were someone watching over the mill, someone who shifted the works to get you back over there on the job when you moved a dangerous distance from your duties. I was never one to believe in spirits, but I knew what made that mill run, and I knew there was no physical explanation for that sudden shift every time I walked near the area by the stairs. Believe me, I tested that phenomenon in every way I could think of. I could tie off the beam and walk around fairly close by for as long as I liked, but as soon as I got to that spot halfway across the mill, *bam!*—it would happen again.

"We did have one other very odd experience. There is a gap as big as a man's fist in the turning radius at the top of the mill; it's a spot where the oak has warped. That gap has to be kept lubricated, and we always did it by stuffing spermaceti candle nubs into the hole. The hollow ran southwest to northeast, so when the blades were east and west, when the mill was sitting right, we'd stuff nubs in there to keep everything going smoothly. We'd ask women to save their spermaceti candle nubs, and we always had a good sackful.

"Well, one night I put in maybe fifty nubs before locking up. I turned the mill once or twice to mash them in, then shut everything down and switched on the alarms.

"The next morning, Anita and I came in, and I climbed up to the third floor, where the turning radius sits, to check on the works. I couldn't believe my eyes. All of the wicks from the candles I had put in the night before were in two little piles on the floor. They were in perfect condition, the wax neatly stripped from each one.

"Now, when you turn the mill after putting the candles in, both wicks and wax get mashed into a sticky residue. I had turned the mill the night before, and not only had these wicks somehow gotten out of the turning radius, but they were still rounded; they had certainly not been flattened. It was just impossible. We do have mice in the mill, but if the mice had managed to extract the wicks from the pulp in the turning radius, which had never happened before, the wicks would have been bent and nibbled. It was just crazy. No one had been in the mill since we locked up the night before. I gathered up a handful of these clean, stripped wicks and brought them down to Anita. We're still marveling over that.

"I loved being the miller. I got to know every inch of that building. For instance, under the stairs are two grooves in the floor planking. Those grooves are very old. They were made by the bottom of a ladder that rested there before the stairs were built. The left groove is worn deeper than the right; there must have been a miller who always started up the ladder with a heavy clump on the left side of the first rung.

"Running that place was a terrific experience, but it was exhausting. One summer I ground seven thousand pounds of cornmeal and had between fourteen and fifteen thousand visitors come through the mill. That's a lot of talking and explaining. And I used to start up the mill, operate it for fifteen minutes, and shut it down for each new crowd of people. It just got to be too much.

"When I ran into those inexplicable shenanigans in the mill, the beam shifting on its own and the piles of clean wicks, I immediately thought of Timothy Swain. Of course, there's no way to prove who or what was responsible, but anyone who was in that building grinding corn by moonlight had to know what he was doing. A nocturnal twirl would be a job for an experienced miller. Timothy Swain owned that mill and died in it. It makes sense that he would still have a finger on the works."

Under the Scallop Shells

"I had a ghost when I was a kid. He never did have a name to him; he was just My Friend. He followed me around, talked to me, sometimes told me things that were going to happen. He wanted me to find something for him. He wanted me to dig something up, and I tried, I really did, but I always got sent back. I just wasn't able to help him.

"We moved into the farmhouse in Polpis when I was ten. My father was caretaking the property for Mr. and Mrs. Hopper, who also owned the big house down the road. The farmhouse is old, and apparently it was common knowledge that there was something odd about it. I can remember Mrs. Hopper's servants asking my mother, a little while after we'd moved, 'How's the old place? How're you folks settling in?'

"My mother and father both knew that the place was haunted. You couldn't help but know. Sometimes you'd hear a group of people arguing in another part of the house, or you'd hear footsteps creaking around upstairs. When the house was empty, when my brother and I were at school and my father was at work, my mother would sometimes walk into the sitting room and find herself overwhelmed by a strong smell of pipe smoke. We used to chain our dog outside, and one day we returned to the house and found the dog locked inside. We had the only key. My brother and I and my parents knew from the beginning that we weren't alone.

"For as long as I can remember, I've known things were going to happen before they occurred; I've known things I didn't know in ordinary terms. As a very young child, I'd sometimes get a vivid mental picture of an accident happening to someone I knew. It was upsetting, and I would run and tell my parents. The very same accident I had seen in my mind's eye would usually occur within the next day or so. It would involve a broken leg or a banged-up car, something like that, and once in a while it would involve someone dying. Second sight is really a burden. I wouldn't wish it on anyone. I've tried to block it all my adult life. I don't go looking for those weird feelings; they come find me on their own.

"Soon after we moved into the farmhouse I began seeing an older man around the place. I wasn't afraid of him; he had a kind face and was always pleasant and friendly to me. He was between sixty and seventy, I'd say, and he was tall, thin, quiet. He looked like a giant, but then I was quite small, and any adult looks enormous when you're that age. He had no beard, and his face was weathered and creased. I can remember the half-circle lines that bracketed his mouth and the laugh lines under his eyes. He wore a plain, dark suit and big, cloddy work boots, the kind a farmer would wear. And he had calloused hands. He looked as solid as any living person.

"I talked to My Friend out loud, and he answered me silently. I wouldn't actually see his mouth moving, but I would hear what he was saying to me. When my mother asked me who I was talking to, I'd say, 'Oh, it's just My Friend, Ma. We're telling each other stories.' She didn't say much, but she never told me I was fibbing, either.

"My Friend would sit outside and talk to me when my brother and I were playing. He'd walk around inside the house with me. At night he'd sit on the end of my bed, and we'd talk about what had happened during the day. He was with me every day for four years, for as long as we lived at the farmhouse.

"I got the feeling that he was looking out for my brother and me, taking special care of us. If we were doing something we weren't allowed to do, he'd say, 'You know you shouldn't do that. You'll get in trouble.' And he was always right.

"At one time my father was talking about getting a boat. My Friend told me right away that my brother would drown if we had a boat. I then began having dreams in which I could see my brother floating on his face in the water and my father reaching over, trying frantically to grab for him. I'd wake up screaming, 'Tom's gonna drown! Tom's gonna drown!' My father was frightened, and he never did get a boat.

"I sat in the backseat of the car when we drove to town, and My Friend would often ride next to me. He'd go just so far down the road, and then he'd be out of the car and I'd see him waving from the side of the road. It was as if he'd only go so far from the property. I once tried to climb out of the car when he got out. I remember my mother yelling and reaching over the backseat to hold on to me.

"My Friend wanted me to do something for him. He told me many times to go to a specific place; it was between the Hoppers' house and the farmhouse, and we kids weren't supposed to go there. There was a huge pile of scallop shells on that spot. Every time I snuck down there and started to dig, someone would find me, one of Mrs. Hopper's servants or my father, and I'd be sent back to the farmhouse. I tried hard to look for what My Friend wanted me to find, but I never had a chance to get very far.

"My brother and I were outside the farmhouse one summer day, playing with Matchbox cars. My Friend came and sat down next to me. Then he said, 'Come with me,' and took me over to a nearby bush. He pointed to a spot on the ground and said, 'Dig right here.' I did, and about three inches under the surface I found a little, old-fashioned engagement ring. It fitted right on my fourth finger. It was a simple ring with a quarter-carat diamond in a gold filigree setting; the stone was encased in gold, in the way they used to set stones. There were no names or initials on the inside. My mother wore it on her little finger until I was eighteen, and then I wore it for years and years. I still have it.

"After we moved to town I never saw My Friend again, but before we left he appeared once to my mother. I'm sure he came to say good-bye. Ma was standing by the front door when she saw him. She said he looked right at her, right into her eyes, and then faded out. She described his clothing and his face.

She'd never seen a spirit before, and she was pretty shocked. For years and years she'd heard me talking to him, but until that happened I don't think she really believed I was talking to anyone but myself.

"I missed My Friend after we moved. He was very good to me, very kind, and I was sorry I never could discover what he wanted me to find under the scallop shells."

My Family Is Here

December 27, 11:00 A.M. The house was cold. Sarah Kierstead looked elegant in two sweaters, pearls, black patent leather shoes. She was wearing no makeup, and her skin was a luminous La Tour white. Her husband, Christian, has a trim beard and the kind of forthright, ladderback posture that automatically straightens the back of anyone facing him. We were at the dining room table. Christian was putting together an intricate set of paper doll's house furniture for their godchild.

Sarah smiled and shrugged. "I grew up with them. It never seemed strange to me. I can remember, as a very young child, asking my mother, 'Who was that walking around the house last night? Who was that banging doors?' My mother simply replied, 'Oh, that was your great-great-grandmother, dear.' Mother was very matter-of-fact about it: there were no explanations; there was no surprise; there was no discussion. I was an only child, and it didn't occur to me that such goings-on might be unusual. The presence in the house of several generations of family members, people who were no longer alive, was always a given. My mother knew when they were around and what they were doing; she could feel it. There was a certain amount of communication. I suppose I have become the same way."

Sarah turned to her husband. "But Christian, why don't we start with your introduction to the house? That's a natural place to begin."

"Sarah and I have been married seven years, and this took place in June the year before we were married." Gesturing with a tiny chaise longue, Christian continued, "We were engaged. Sarah was lecturing in Kentucky, I was between semesters, and she sent me to Nantucket ahead of her. She had told me nothing in great detail about her family history, and she had mentioned nothing about presences in the house.

"It was my first time on the island. I arrived late in the afternoon and took a taxi from the airport. I picked up the spare key from Jim Carr, who lived down the street, and went to open up the house.

"It was getting dark. Sarah had unplugged most of the lamps and draped furniture and paintings with sheets, so I went around the first floor turning some lights on and removing covers from the furniture. I went to the supermarket, then came back and fixed something to eat. I was just starting up the stairs when I had a strong sense, a sudden sureness, that someone was up there. I *knew* the house was empty. I guess I just stood still. And then an authoritative voice with a crisp British accent came out of the darkness above: 'And who are you? What are you doing here?' It was an old woman. My mind ran in place for a moment, and then I did the only thing I could do: I responded. Without moving or even looking up, I said, 'I am a friend of Sarah's, and she will be arriving tomorrow morning on the plane.' I then turned and walked into the bedroom downstairs and shut the door. I did not go upstairs that night.

"I didn't sleep well, and I awoke to find that there was no hot water. I couldn't shave. I couldn't take a shower. I knew the heater was on, but there was simply no hot water at all. I went to meet Sarah at the plane, and I know I looked like hell. ('Yes, when I saw him I did wonder who I was marrying!') I told Sarah that there was no hot water. She just started to laugh. She laughed and laughed. I then told her about the voice coming from upstairs. She said, 'Oh, that was my great-great-grandmother, Deborah Coffin. Or I suppose it could have been Aunt Susie.' She seemed very amused by the whole thing. I said, 'Well, okay, so are you going to tell me what's going on?' She said, 'Let's get home and get the water straightened out and we'll talk.'

"When we got to the house she called Frank Estes, who has taken care of three generations of Sarah's family. He went down to the cellar, kicked the heater a couple of times, and, sure enough, it started up. He grinned. Sarah grinned. After he had gone, Sarah and I went upstairs and sat down in the living room."

"That's right," Sarah added. "I took his hand and said, 'Christian—when my father was courting my mother, he came and stayed in the house. The hot water was out the next morning. Some time after my mother died, my father was courting another woman. She came to stay at the house. The next morning, the hot water was out. And now us. We are number three.'

"Yes, Christian got quite an introduction to the clan. You see, my family is all dead. Our family line is a slender one. I grew up, as I mentioned before, with the accepted presence in the household of various relatives who could not be seen but who could be felt and who manifested themselves occasionally. And it really shouldn't be surprising; the house is still theirs in many ways, for their photographs, journals, treasures, furniture are all still here. I have their china, their ivory, their fans, their calling cards, their silver, their personal odds and ends. And I have always felt a closeness to them, as my mother did. I am pleased to have them around. Thus, I sent Christian to the house to be 'looked over,' to be approved."

"Quite an honor," said Christian dryly. "I survived. That same year, a friend and I returned to the house, without Sarah. I had told Arthur of my experience with Deborah Coffin, of the hot water tradition, and of Sarah's absolute acceptance of the existence of known presences in the house. He was a rather conventional character and didn't believe a word of it.

"One night we noticed a big wet spot on the Oriental carpet upstairs. There was no pipe nearby, no leak from the ceiling. It hadn't rained. The spot was there when we went to bed, and it was still just as wet in the morning. I called Sarah. She wasn't concerned, sensing that it was probably connected with the house. Arthur pooh-poohed it, insisting there must be a simple physical explanation.

"Later that day, while we were sitting in the dining room, the light clicked on by itself in the kitchen. Arthur insisted that the bulb must be loose. Fine.

"Arthur fell in love with Nantucket, and the day before he left he went downtown and bought three paintings. I was mowing the back lawn that afternoon when Arthur rushed out of the house looking wild-eyed. 'Where were you? Were you out here a few minutes ago?' 'Well, yes. You can see that I've been mowing . . .' Arthur said he had been indoors ten minutes earlier, looking for a cardboard box to pack his paintings in. He didn't see anything around the house, so he went down in the cellar. The stairs are very narrow and steep, and there's just room for one person to walk. He said he had a 'creepy' feeling suddenly, and turned around and hurried up the stairs. There, on one of the top steps, was a cardboard carton of just the right size. It had not been there a few moments earlier. Arthur couldn't have stepped over it, for it filled the stairwell. He picked up the box and tore out into the yard. I said, 'Well? Did you say thank you?'

"At Christmas time we were back in the house. I was here in the dining room at the head of the table, carving a ham. Sarah was in the kitchen with a guest. From where I was standing, I could see both the mirror on the wall clock to my right and the mirror in the corner cabinet on the far left. When I look in the clock mirror from that position, I can see a reflection of the mirror in the corner cabinet. While I was tackling the ham, something moved in my peripheral vision. I saw, in the clock mirror, the reflection of a person. I glanced up quickly, expecting to see Sarah, but the room was empty. I looked directly at the clock mirror (this all took place in a matter of one or two seconds) and saw an image, in the reflection of the corner mirror, of a woman just walking past the end of the dining room table. She had gray hair pulled back tightly in a bun, a shawl of some kind over her shoulders, and a dark, long-sleeved dress. I missed a direct look at the front of her face, but I saw her from about here, from her cheekbone back. In other words, I saw nothing when I looked directly into the room, but I saw, in the clock mirror, the reflection of her reflection as she passed by the corner mirror.

"I was pretty shaken up. I went right into the kitchen and told Sarah. She said, 'Why, that's Nanna! I had a feeling, as I was standing here, that she was in there with you.'

"And that was the end of the discussion until the following day. The next morning Sarah brought out a photograph album from one of the desks. 'Do you see anyone familiar?' she asked. I must say, I was taken aback. Because there she was. I recognized her immediately. The hair, the shape of her face, the shawl: it was the older woman I had seen the evening before."

Sarah continued, "Two or three years before Christian and I were courting, I had a couple visiting me here. They are friends from California. Bob is a physics professor, Claire runs a classical radio station. They are very much city people, and not the sort to have encountered presences. And, I might add, not the sort to believe. So I didn't warn them.

"We were supposed to come to the house together, but I got called away at the last moment on business. I sent them up ahead of me, drawing them a diagram showing where to find sheets, how to turn on the heat, and so on.

"When I arrived a couple of days later, they were rather quiet about the house, but did say that they'd been enjoying the island. It's the custom of our family to make a really fine quahog chowder as a way of welcoming guests. The recipe has been passed down through the generations, and it takes three days to prepare. I can remember my mother and grandmother making it together when I was a child.

"I started in on the chowder. The first day it needs to be beaten, on the stove, every fifteen minutes or so. So I beat the chowder all day, and before we went to bed I put it in the refrigerator. The next morning, Claire came into the kitchen and said, 'Why, Sarah! You must be exhausted. We heard you up beating the chowder all night long. We also heard you bustling up and down the stairs. Couldn't you sleep?'

"I had to confess to Claire that I hadn't left my bedroom. I had slept like a log the whole night. As her eyes widened, I explained to her that it was probably just my great-great-grandmother and that it was quite a normal thing, nothing to get upset about. She said, 'Oh, Sarah! I'm afraid we called the police on your grandmother when we first got to the house!'

"Bob and Claire hadn't known how to tell me this, but during their first night here they awoke to the sounds of someone walking around upstairs. They heard doors slam and sharp, clear footsteps in the hall.

"They had been very careful to lock up before going to bed. Bob reached for the phone and called the police. When two patrolmen arrived, Claire and Bob and the cops went through every corner of the house, but found no evidence of a prowler.

"After the police were gone, Bob said, 'I need a drink. This is just too much.' I had told him that the liquor was all in the cellar under a white sheet at the foot of the stairs. He turned on the light and went down.

"Ten minutes before, he and Claire and the two policemen had looked through the cellar. No liquor bottles had been visible. This time, Bob got to the foot of the stairs and found himself looking at a full bottle of whiskey. He was sure it had not been there a few minutes before. It was some distance from the corner where the liquor was kept.

"He reached down, grabbed the bottle, said 'Most kind! Thank you!' and galloped up the stairs.

"I must tell you about our wedding. We got married in the house, and planned the entire ceremony and reception in the style of an 1830 celebration. I even, to the horror of some costume experts at the Smithsonian, wore my great-grandmother's wedding gown. (This dress had been made in Paris; it didn't belong to one of my Nantucket grandmothers.) We had a marvelous time. There was a considerable amount of champagne and wine consumed. There were thirty-two people at the reception, all close friends, and every one, I believe, had heard about the presences in the house.

"When we were drinking toasts in the dining room, Christian poured a fresh glass of champagne and said a toast to 'those members of the family who are present in spirit but who cannot be seen.' We put the glass down by the side of the wedding cake.

"After that toast, the entire party went into the living room. We were about to start off the dancing when Christian looked back into the dining room for some reason and said, 'Sarah. The glass is empty.' And so it was. The glass was sitting in the exact spot where I had put it down moments before, but the champagne had been drained. We could tell it had not been moved because there was only the one ring imprint left on the starched tablecloth.

"Later that night, after we had gone up to bed, several friends were sitting around the fire downstairs and swore that they saw a woman's face, a friendly face, in the flames. At any rate, I feel sure that my family was pleased about our marriage. And they were most definitely there.

"One year not too long ago, I lent the house to a colleague for Thanksgiving weekend. Remembering Claire and Bob's experience, I forewarned him about my relatives. I requested that he not, under any circumstances, call the police on my great-great-grandmother. He said he had experienced phenomena of this kind before and wasn't concerned; however, he was not going to say anything about it to his three children.

"Monday morning at 9:01 my office phone rang. It was my friend.

"On their first night in the house, the three children were put to bed in the middle bedroom upstairs. At breakfast the next morning they had said, 'Dad, who was the lady who talked to us last night?' When he looked surprised, they explained that she came into their bedroom after they were all in bed and asked them in a strange accent what each of their names were and what they were doing in the house. They had answered politely, assuming she was also a guest. She then turned and left the room and they went to sleep. She was as solid as could be and had a long-sleeved, floor-length gray dress on. I suppose the children just thought it was a robe. They weren't frightened; they were just curious about who she was.

"I feel sure that was Deborah Coffin who talked with the children. Her maiden name was Bishop. After she married Zaccheus North Coffin in 1835, they moved into this house. The core of the building goes back to 1802, but Zaccheus Coffin had it done over and expanded in the Greek Revival mode that was popular in those days.

"Deborah Bishop's family was from Philadelphia; they were sugar merchants. Deborah spent fifty-nine years in this house and died in 1904 at the respectable age of eighty-nine. Zaccheus was a seventh-generation Nantucketer who distinguished himself as a commander in the Civil War. He came back badly wounded. You can see from the photograph in the downstairs bedroom that he is missing an arm. Come; I'll show you. His musket and his crutch are both leaning against the wall in the corner here. Feel the weight of this musket. Can you believe they had to carry that on horseback?

"Zaccheus and Deborah were my great-great-grandparents, and they had two children, Susannah and John. Susannah Pinkham Coffin, otherwise known as Aunt Susie, was born in 1836. She married Frederick P. Dover, of New York, and I know she was living in the house at the time of her death in 1915. John Gage Coffin was born in 1837. He married Eleanor Chase, and they had three children. After Aunt Susie died, the house went to John and Eleanor Coffin's daughter Emily. We called her Aunt Em. Aunt Em never married, and lived in the house until she died in 1942. Her sister, Cora Macy Winston, whom I always knew as Nanna, then lived here until her death in 1958. She was my grandmother. Her only child was my mother, Sarah North, who married Francis Dale. And then there was me.

"It's a matriarchal line; the house has always been left to women. First there was Deborah, who quite definitely ruled her roost. Then there was Aunt Susie, then Aunt Em, then Nanna, then my mother. They were powerful women, all of them, within the framework society allowed them.

"Deborah Coffin was fiery and independent and spoke out openly on women's rights. She once lost her temper and threw her bonnet into the fire at Quaker meeting. I have a marvelous journal of hers in the front parlor. She records what she did each day, who she called on, what transpired in the community. Aunt Em worked hard to support the arts and poetry. She was very musical. My grandmother Nanna was a bluestocking. She worked for the vote and the right to smoke. And my mother contributed much time and thought to the community here. She was one of the founding members of the then-controversial Historic Districts Commission in the fifties.

"I am the first woman in the family to work professionally, but I am not, by any means, the first determined female. I can blame it all on my relatives."

"Oh, Sarah," said Christian, reaching for the scissors. "We forgot the business about your father. Do you want to mention that?"

"Sure."

"Sarah's father was a distinguished general during the Second World War. He was known, for the rest of his life, as 'the General.' He often carried a riding crop, and Sarah says that he had a distinctive way of walking that resulted in an odd duet of boots and crop.

"The summer after we were married, we were late one day in getting up. We had guests in the house and should really have been downstairs fixing breakfast. Suddenly, we both heard a *step-step-slap*, *step-step-slap* coming up the stairs.

"Sarah said with delight, 'It's Papa! It's my father!' The tone of his step said 'Goddammit, get up. Don't you have things to take care of?' It was very funny. When we opened the bedroom door, we saw no one, but we had most definitely heard him coming. And the dog, who was in with us, had jumped up and barked wildly at the bedroom door as the steps approached.

"A couple of other odd happenings seemed to involve the General. We had a guest, Laura, who was downstairs reading one morning before Sarah and I got up. She was over on the far side of the living room. You can see the front door from where she was sitting.

"When I came downstairs with the dog, Laura said, 'Oh, you're taking him out again?' I said, 'No, Laura, I'm just getting up.' She then explained that she had just seen a man with a cap (I usually wear a hat) slip out the door with a dog. She had heard noises and seen the flick of the dog's tail as they stepped out and shut the door. When she realized I hadn't been downstairs at all, she shrugged and said, 'Well. I must have dreamed it.'

"The next morning, Pam, another friend who was staying with us, was reading the paper in the living room. She happened to be sitting where Laura had been sitting the day before. I came downstairs with the dog, and we had a repeat performance of the same situation. She swore she had just seen a man go out with the dog a few minutes earlier. The General wore a cap and usually walked Sarah's dog Caleb, who looked quite a bit like the dog we have now. Perhaps the General just felt I was tardy in getting the dog out and took matters into his own hands.

"The interesting thing is that Laura had not mentioned her experience of the previous day to Pam. After Laura found out that I hadn't been downstairs at all, she decided that what she had seen never really happened.

"It's very hard for most people to accept an occurrence they don't understand," Sarah added. "Now, just for the record, I'd like to make one thing clear: the presences we have described today are members of my family and must be treated with respect. I feel very strongly about that. We do not use the word 'ghost' in referring to them. Although I cannot see them, they are around in the house; in fact, the path that Deborah most often takes, when I am aware of her walking, is through the dining room here, up the front stairs, and into the middle bedroom. That was the room in which my colleague's children saw a woman. Nanna stayed downstairs in her old age, and she goes through the dining room (where Christian saw her) and into the borning room over here, which was her bedroom. My family, although no longer alive, are very much with me in this house. Although they were all buried at Arlington, everyone seems to have come home."

Janet Rivard:

"I've been house-sitting this fall for Sarah and Christian. My four children are all grown and out of the nest, and I'm in the process of selling my house on the mainland and moving to Nantucket.

"I wouldn't call myself a believer, not having had any dramatic ghost encounters of my own, but I am open-minded. Before I moved in, Sarah warned me that there are 'presences' here.

"When I was getting settled in, I had to go back and forth between here and my old apartment, lugging boxes full of papers and books, my typewriter, suitcases, and all my other belongings. I had brought my phone and answering machine with me so that I could hold on to my own number. I plugged in the machine as soon as I brought it into the house.

"On my first night here, I switched the machine on and began playing back messages. There seemed to be six hang-ups in a row. I rewound the tape and turned up the volume. The first four bleeps had small noises on them; they sounded like someone preparing to speak, you know, like an intake of breath, a throat-clearing, or the indefinite noises a child will make while trying to figure out what to say. It was hard to tell, too, if they weren't just static on the machine. Finally, after the fifth bleep I could hear an older woman's voice whisper, 'This is Mrs. Dover,' and then the message ended. The sixth bleep seemed to be a hang-up again.

"Sarah called just as I finished playing back my tape, and because it had just happened, I mentioned the answering machine messages. I told her about the whisper, and commented on how strange it was; I didn't, and still don't, know a Mrs. Dover. Now, remember, this was my phone number, not Sarah's. When I mentioned Mrs. Dover, Sarah laughed. 'Oh, my,' she said. 'Mrs. Dover was my great-great-aunt.' "

Old and Young

"Everything was wrong with this house. The basement flooded every other week, the heat went out, the toilet backed up, the refrigerator broke, and the kitchen was a Betty Furness aqua and pink that almost made you ill. But it was cheap.

"My friend Cyrus Hall and I were in our twenties. We were both new to the island, and neither of us had any money. When we located the house we thought we'd found a perfect winter rental; a seedy living situation on wild Nantucket was a definite badge of distinction.

"It was the fall of 1972 when we moved in. On our second day there, I was coming home from work at 5:30 and saw an old man with a gray coat and a gray fedora hat. He was standing by the front door and seemed to be fumbling with his key. I thought to myself, Oh, great. Some old geezer lives here too, and we won't be able to have parties. By the time I'd parked the car, he was gone. I assumed he'd gone into the house.

"The building had been divided into three apartments; I'd met the kids living in the other two, and assumed that this guy belonged to a fourth living area tucked away someplace in the back. I didn't give it much thought.

"When we had been in our apartment for a week or so, Cyrus came into the kitchen one morning with a funny look on his face. He told me that he'd woken up in the night to see a man with a hat on standing at the foot of his bed. Startled, he'd sat straight up, and the image had vanished.

"One night I also woke up and saw a shape in the darkness. My eyesight isn't terribly good, and I assumed that it was my coat hanging on the back of the door. I could see the shoulders and the general shape of a person, but really thought it was just clothing on a hanger and maybe a hat thrown over the hook. I was groggy, so I rolled over and went back to sleep. In the morning I found that there was nothing hanging on my door. I remember that green feeling in the pit of my stomach when I realized that I didn't know what I'd seen, but I *knew* I had seen it.

"I noticed the old man a couple of other times, always when I was getting home at dusk. I only saw him from my car; he was always gone by the time I got to the front sidewalk. I don't remember correlating the sight of the old man at the door with the figures we had seen inside at night.

"One morning I was talking with one of the girls who were renting the lower apartment. I thought of the old guy and asked if she knew anything about him. She gave me a funny look and said that there was no older person living in the house.

"My girlfriend, Jody, moved in during the winter. She didn't have a job and was alone during the day while Cyrus and I were at work. She didn't know a soul on Nantucket, but she repeatedly heard someone calling her name. She went to the door again and again, puzzled, but there was never anyone there.

In early spring, a friend of Jody's came for the weekend and Cyrus, thoughtful guy that he was, gave the guest his room and planned to sleep on the living room couch. He was sitting up reading the paper, after the rest of us had gone to bed, and something caught his eye in the corner of the room. Looking up, he saw the faint silhouette of a man with a hat. It was more an outline than a solid shape and seemed to be moving slowly toward him. He said he really couldn't believe what was going on, and just sat there, more curious than afraid.

"And then something horrible happened. He felt this shape go into him, or so he said, and he felt himself drowning in a wash of ugly, angry, violent emotion. He had a strong urge to go into my room and attack Jody and me, to do something physically harmful to us. It sounds laughable as I'm telling you this, but I guess it was pretty terrifying at the time. He jumped up from the sofa and ran into the bathroom and started splashing cold water on his face and neck. When he looked up in the mirror, holding a towel, he said that a hideous face was 'coming out of his.' He claimed that something horrendous, inside his body, was looking out at him.

"Now, we'd had a humdrum, dull evening and made something hallucinogenic like Rice-a-Roni for dinner. Cyrus was straight, and he didn't do drugs; the most any of us did was drink wine and beer.

"Not knowing what else to do, he turned on all the lights and went to the kitchen and made coffee. He said he sat at the table and drank a full pot and smoked cigarette after cigarette. By dawn, he felt this presence leave him. It was there one moment, an outrageous urge inside him, and then it was gone. He knew the moment it left, and he was okay. Exhausted, he laid down on the couch and slept most of the day.

"That afternoon he was in the kitchen, telling Jody and her friend about what had happened the night before. I was in the bedroom taking a nap.

"I woke up to feel a tremendous pressure on my neck and the back of my head. I had to struggle to get myself out from under it—it was as if someone had put a sofa cushion on top of me and was leaning on it with all their weight. When I got myself to a sitting position, I jumped out of bed and ran into the kitchen, and that's when I heard about Cyrus's experience of the previous night.

"By then all of us had the spooks, and Cyrus and Jody and I couldn't wait to move out of the place. Nothing much happened for a few weeks, and then, shortly before the lease was up, we were sitting around in the kitchen with some friends and someone suggested we have a séance. It was one of those 'Yeah! Great idea!' party situations.

"We had a Ouija board, and four of us sat down around a table. None of us had ever used one of those things before. We did seem to contact something. The pointer spelled out that the spirit was that of a girl who had died in an explosion. That was scary, and we quit right there. We had had at least two bottles of wine that night, and by the next morning the whole business looked pretty silly.

"In 1974 I met a couple working for the Historical Association who mentioned that they had just left a miserably uncomfortable rental. She told me it was on the same street as the apartment Cyrus and I had lived in two years before. It turned out to be the same place. I asked her if she'd noticed anything odd. She said she hadn't, really, except that the house just 'felt bad,' and that she had repeatedly seen a man in a gray coat and a fedora hat outside their back door. She could see him through the kitchen window. Every time she walked over to the door and opened it, no one was there.

"Years later, I was doing research in the Historical Association's Peter Foulger Library and came across a box of old *Inquirer and Mirror* newspapers. I was browsing through them, curious to see the hot items of the 1950s and 1960s, and a small article caught my eye. You can look it up, but please change all the names; I don't want to upset anyone. The article stated that a young Nantucket woman had been killed in an explosion somewhere down South. It then went on to say that she had grown up in the house Cyrus and I had rented in 1972."

Quakers

"I was aware of a mother and a father and a boy of about fourteen. The woman wore a long, simple dress and a Quaker bonnet, and the man was in a dark suit. They were sitting in front of the fireplace in the front room, the adults in chairs and the boy on a low sofa or bench of some kind. I couldn't see them in everyday terms, but I could see them inside of myself; I knew they were there, and that they were reacting to my presence in the house."

Mrs. Abigail Halstead lives outside of Washington, D.C., with her husband, John. The Halsteads and their children and grandchildren have been spending summers on Nantucket for many years.

Mrs. Halstead went on: "I hesitate to tell this story, because it makes me sound quite crazy, but you're obviously used to hearing people talk about these things. I've known I was what you'd call 'psychic' from the time I was quite young. I've never pursued it or tried to develop that side of myself; quite frankly, I think it's scary and confusing. You could get lost delving into that other side of life. Oh yes, I am absolutely positive that ghosts exist. If there's anything in a house, I can always feel it, or perhaps it would be more accurate to say that it always seems to feel me.

"I bought our present house in 1960. It was built in 1735 and had been moved in to town from Sherburne, which as you know was the earliest settlement on the island. I knew they were there on my first night in the house. I could feel them most clearly in that front room; at times they were all there, sitting by the hearth, and at other times the room was empty.

"They seemed to be a Quaker family and had a stiff and rather forbidding aura to them. They behaved in the way one would imagine Quakers would act

if someone uninvited moved into their home. The parents were stern and formal and quite dignified. I never saw them move. The son, on the other hand,
followed me around downstairs and did a couple of naughty fourteen-year-old
things.

"An interesting aside involves my neighbors, the Thomases, who helped me
out in the house during those first few weeks. I was there alone, living in the
back bedroom, and they helped me move things and plan needed renovations
and so on. They knew, walking into that front room, when there was something there; they couldn't see anything, but my sense and their sense of when
the room was 'occupied' always coincided.

"I was locking the front door one day, and I could feel that young boy
behind me. The door has an old-fashioned lock with a knob that you have to
set in place and turn in a certain way. It's a very deliberate series of movements,
and the knob can't slip out or turn on its own. Well, I locked the door, and it
slowly unlocked before my eyes. I did it again. He did it again. We went
through this performance one more time, and then I said, very firmly, 'That's
enough of that.' I locked the door, and it stayed that way.

"My brother was visiting me during that first spring in the house, and I had
been telling him about the Quakers and about their prankish little boy. He
pooh-poohed my stories and was rather condescending about the whole thing.
Well, I could feel, as we were talking, that the young boy was near us. So I said
to my brother, 'Well, why don't you try the door and see what happens?' He
walked over and locked the door. It was carefully unlocked, the knob turning
and moving slowly out on its own. He said, 'Well, that is funny. I just can't
understand it.' He did it again, and the door again unlocked itself. I must say
I was pleased. I then said something like, 'All right, please leave that knob alone
now,' and my brother locked it again, and that was that. He mumbled something about 'must be an explanation,' but he did look rather taken aback.

"I felt the young boy upstairs only once. I had a guest, and I had arranged
all sorts of bath oils and powders and soaps for her on a low shelf around the

tub. Perhaps he thought I had overdone it, for the entire shelf-full was swept into the tub with a tremendous clatter. It was a bit irritating and alarmed my guest.

"When the Quakers didn't leave and I had been in the house for several months, I decided that we should have a little talk. I wanted everyone who stayed in the house to feel comfortable, and that required some adjustment. I waited until I could feel the Quakers in the room, and then I went and sat down across from them on the other side of the hearth. I said, out loud, 'I know this was once your home, but now it's time for you to leave. I love this house and I'm taking good care of it. I want this to be a happy home. I don't want it to be a scary place for my family. This house is in good hands, and I want you to go now.' I was very firm. And, quite honestly, that was the last I felt of them.

"Over the years, I have heard of a number of other haunted houses on Nantucket. It isn't uncommon here. At one time we were staying on Academy Lane, and there was a house down the street that very definitely had a ghost in it. I remember that one of our children saw a lady's face in the window. I was also told about a house somewhere near the intersection of India and Gardner—supposedly, the sounds of a party could be heard downstairs when the house was empty. There was a story about a husband and wife having a dreadful row at that party, and the woman running blindly out into the street and being hit and killed by a car. The echoes of that evening could be heard in the house for many years after this dreadful thing happened.

"There are spirits in our house near Washington, which is also very old, and I've run across ghosts in houses in other parts of the country. It doesn't generally surprise me, and I try not to pay too much attention unless it's something that interferes with present-day living. It happens, I say 'hmm' to myself, and continue folding the blanket or walking up the stairs or doing whatever I happen to be doing."

Life's Strange Happenings

We arranged to meet at the Brotherhood. It is a wet Sunday, one of those almost-here spring days when coats are too warm and sweaters not enough. Gray droplets cling to the windows of the restaurant. Jack Decatur is sitting at a table by the fire. He has a dark beret, black curly hair, quiet glasses, and a plaid shirt.

"I'm one of those chronic students; I love to learn. I came to Nantucket ten years ago as an undergraduate studying ethology at the University of Massachusetts Field Station in Quaise. I spent seven years there, off and on, working summers and later doing graduate studies in the evolution and ecology of fish behavior. I have yet to hand in the final draft of my thesis; meanwhile, I've gotten into antiques.

"I've always been a history buff, and I had a couple of friends who were doing legwork for the auctioneer Rafael Osona. I went to one of Osona's auctions when I had nothing to do one Saturday, and I was hooked. Rafael flies: he's knowledgeable, he's perceptive, he's fast. He's very good at what he does. I've been working for him for seven years now, and I've learned a tremendous amount. I accompany him when he does appraisals or house calls, I help him when he goes off-island to pick up consignments, I lug, I pack, I fill in while he's away during the winter. He handles an impressive volume of antiques in his Nantucket auctions.

"I've been on the island year-round for three years. Finding a place to live is a real problem, and I've spent some time sleeping on friends' sofas while scratching around for a rental. The following story took place last fall.

"I had been camping out in a chilly garage apartment, and Holly S., who was house-sitting, offered me an upstairs bedroom. I was thrilled; sleeping in an old Nantucket house is always an adventure, rather like sleeping in a Hawthorne novel, and this building looked like it held some tales.

"Holly told me she had felt frightened at night in this house. She said it was nothing specific; she just hadn't felt comfortable. She was glad to have some company.

"On my first night in the house, I slept soundly. I was awakened in the morning by a tickling sensation on my eyelids. I would roll over; it would go away. I would doze off; it would come back. I opened my eyes and saw a couple of flies buzzing around the bed. It's too cold for houseflies, I thought sleepily.

"I lay on my back, stretched, and watched the sun making patterns on the far wall. I could hear breakfast sounds coming from downstairs: loud men's voices, the *clink-clink* of china, chairs scraping on the floor, the clatter of pots and a frying pan on the gas range. It was rowdy and cheery-sounding, and made me think of a bunch of guys staying in a hunting lodge. Holly didn't seem to be there. I could distinguish the voices of three different men.

"I lay in bed for fifteen or twenty minutes, just enjoying the room, listening, waiting for a whiff of coffee or bacon to drift up the stairs. I did think the party was a little surprising, and I wondered who had come for breakfast while Holly was still asleep. I was hungry, but couldn't smell cooking. Finally, I sat up and stretched. When my feet hit the floor, the house went absolutely still. No sounds from the kitchen, no cheery voices, just the whir of a truck turning the corner. I sat there for a moment, my ears straining for the smallest noise. Feeling suddenly chilled, I hurried into my jeans and crept downstairs. Holly's bedroom door was still shut; she was not awake. The kitchen was empty and clean.

"I heard those men in the kitchen every morning for the next ten days. The sounds were pleasant and boisterous and very natural. And the flies: I was always awakened by flies walking on my face, although they were never in my room, or for that matter anywhere else in the house, at any other time of day.

As soon as I was up and dressed, the flies would be gone. And no matter how quiet I was, the moment my bare feet touched the floor, the party in the kitchen would evaporate.

"Holly never heard anything in the kitchen, and she never saw any flies. A month later, she was called off-island for two weeks and I stayed on in the house.

"As soon as she was gone, the breakfast noises became louder and borderline raucous. And I found myself feeling jumpy and watchful.

"The house has a back staircase that Holly and I referred to as 'the crooked stairs.' They sit in the oldest part of the building, and have pie-shaped treads that twist their way in a steep, narrow spiral from the first floor to the second. There is also a newer stairwell in the house, one that was obviously put in with a nineteenth-century addition. These stairs run straight up in the conventional manner. My bedroom was near the door to the attic and the top of the crooked stairs.

"When alone in the house, I felt very uncomfortable walking past the attic door. I felt nervous, close to afraid, although I tried not to admit it to myself. I had a nasty feeling that something wanted to push me down those crooked stairs. When I went up into the attic, everything felt fine; the bad feeling returned only as I stood at the top of the stairs with my back to the attic door.

"I instinctively began to avoid the back stairs. I made a long detour up the front staircase, the straight stairs, every time I needed something from my room.

"I heard the breakfast crew many times over that two-week period. I kind of enjoyed them. At any rate, they weren't frightening. But the bad feeling in the house began to spread. When I first noticed it, it was localized, centered around the crooked stairs, but now I could be sitting downstairs in the living room and I'd suddenly feel afraid, threatened. I'm the first to say it could have been my imagination, 'an undigested bit of beef,' but whatever the cause, it was hard to live with. I found myself avoiding the entire house with the exception of the kitchen and my bedroom. I'd cook my dinner, read the paper or write letters down at the table there, and run straight up the new staircase and jump into bed.

The door to my bedroom, the one that opened near the top of the crooked stairs, refused to stay closed. I would shut the door and turn my back; minutes later, the door would be standing wide open. It has a snug latch, and it won't open unless pressure is applied to the handle. I finally gave up entirely and left the door open day and night.

"As soon as Holly returned, I moved back, with relief, into my chilly and impersonal garage. When it came time for her to leave the house, Holly called me up and asked if I would come over and help her clean.

"I vacuumed the first floor while she was running around dusting furniture and changing beds. She then sent me up to the second floor. I felt very uncomfortable, but I lugged the vacuum up and did a real rush job, working as fast as I could. I had a strong feeling that I was not welcome in that building. When I was about two-thirds of the way down the new stairs, working from the top, something made me look up. I found myself staring at a tall, stocky woman. She had gray hair pulled back in a bun and was wearing something like a floor-length nightgown. She was completely solid, and she seemed stern, almost cross. We looked each other right in the eye. She had a petulant, 'Missed a spot, you idiot!' expression. And then she was gone. There was no fading out; she was there, and then she wasn't.

"David Fielding, whose parents owned the house, lives a couple of doors down the street. You might want to talk to him. And Betina Frye, who bought the house two years ago, told me she and her family have had some odd times there."

David Fielding:

"When my parents bought the house in 1960, it was a real mess. Paint chips the size of pancakes, missing shingles, a yard choked with weeds: the house was a horror show.

"My parents cleaned things up but didn't do anything major to the structure of the building. The oldest part of the house is said to date back to 1740 or so, and was supposedly moved from Sherburne. An addition built in the early nineteenth century changed the original lean-to into a full house, and then the rest of the building was added around 1840 or 1850, at which time it was converted into a two-family dwelling. Of course, those apartment divisions were taken down many years ago, but you can still see two separate front entrances, one on each street.

"My mother was *formidable*, as they say in France, and my father was deaf, so they probably weren't ideal conduits for a ghostly type of experience. My mother did tell me that she heard boots walking in the main hall, but she didn't elaborate on it. She treated it like faulty plumbing; it was not an interesting topic to bring up, not something worthy of a great deal of discussion. My daughter Paula spent some time living in that house with her grandparents.

"Well, what do you know? I wasn't expecting her, but here's Paula now."

On being asked about the house, Paula said, "I do remember one quite dramatic incident. This was a very real thing; it was not in any way an imagined feeling.

"I was alone in the house, sitting in the kitchen reading at about 8:30 on a summer evening. My dog was lying on the floor under the table.

"We both heard someone in heavy shoes walking through one of the bedrooms and then coming down the front stairs and into the hall. It was definitely not the random creaking of an old house; it was the cadence, the measured rhythm, of a person going down steps. My dog sat right up, sniffing and listening, and I got up my courage and went to the kitchen door, trying to make as much noise as possible. To my relief, the steps stopped as soon as I poked my head into the hall."

The house has a bashful look to it. Towering at the intersection of two narrow streets, the building steps heavily on a ribbon of sidewalk; one thinks of a large, shy person who has been given a push from behind. The interior is an architectural muddle. Toward the front of the house, the rooms are formal and straight-backed and have surprisingly high ceilings. As one walks north through the building, ceilings dip and sag, door frames slump, floor boards grow tipsy and garrulous. One feels there are two distinct poles in the house: the crooked stairs, at the back, and the newer stairwell, at the front.

Betina Frye:

"My husband Bill and I have owned the house for two years now. We live on Long Island, but I'm up here all summer and whenever I can manage it during the fall and winter.

"The following event took place just after we bought the house. My mother and I were up here alone for a long weekend in March.

"My mother is a cool, clinical person. She's extremely level-headed, and absolutely not one to dwell on unexplained happenings. I was sleeping downstairs in my bedroom, and my mother was upstairs in the room directly over mine. We went to bed around eleven, and I went right to sleep.

"I woke up at 11:45 to the sound of a woman singing operatic scales. The singing stopped abruptly, and the next thing I heard was the sound of arguing coming from my mother's bedroom. It was rather loud and insistent in tone. I froze; I was paralyzed. I knew that my mother and I were alone in the house, and yet I could hear a man and a woman fighting in her room. Occasionally I heard the even sound of my mother's voice. And I'm ashamed to say I didn't leap out of bed or even squawk; I'd be a failure in a real emergency.

"After what seemed like forever, the voices stopped abruptly. There was a moment of silence, and then my mother called out to me, sounding quite calm. I popped up in bed and shrieked, 'Oh my God, Mom! What's going on up there? Are you all right?' My mother hollered back that she was fine and that she'd tell me about it in the morning. I can remember her saying, 'You'll never believe this.'

"We were both up early. My mother told me that she couldn't sleep the night before and was doing the *New York Times* crossword puzzle in bed until quite late. Shortly after she took off her glasses and turned out the light, she heard voices. She peered through the darkness and made out two figures on the other side of the room; it was a clear night, and there was some light coming in from the moon. The man she recognized immediately. She said it was her father, who had died when she was twelve years old. Crazy as it sounds, she was quite sure of that. The other figure was a woman, and the form wasn't as clearly defined as that of the man, but she could make out a round, solid figure and hair pulled back off the face in a bun or twist. The woman said she was looking for Margaret (that isn't my mother's name), and then she said she wanted my mother to come with her. The male figure then insisted that my mother stay here, and the two of them argued back and forth. My mother said something at some point; I don't know if it was 'Hello, Father' or 'Yes, I'll stay here' or what. She really doesn't remember, the whole thing was so kooky. And then, quite suddenly, they were gone. That was when my mother called down to me.

"Mom was as frightened as I was, although I guess she handled it better. As we admitted to each other in the morning, we had stayed in our respective bedrooms because neither one of us wanted to walk through the dark house or invite any other weird appearances. I mean, can you believe it? You're driving on the Long Island Expressway in the morning, you stop at some place like McDonald's for lunch, and late that same night you're listening to two ghosts fighting. It doesn't fit at all with the world most of us live in.

"When I related this to David Fielding some time later, he said that he has a sister, Frances, who is an opera singer and lives in Europe. She is very much alive and used to practice in this house. I don't know if Frances ties in in any way with the opera scales I heard that night, but I think the connection is interesting.

"The next thing that happened involved my husband, Bill. We had come to the island alone, a couple of months after my mother's visit. He woke up early one morning to hear a man walking around upstairs. He heard a heavy stride moving across one of the bedrooms and down the old staircase. He then heard the steps clumping through the kitchen, into the sitting room, and toward our bedroom. He was concerned, and hopped out of bed and opened the door. Nothing. No sound. I slept through all of this. Bill went back to bed.

"We had a series of odd incidents that we didn't pay much attention to. I mean, what do you do with an experience like that? All you can do is tuck it in the file of 'Life's Strange Happenings' and carry on.

"We have had trouble, all along, with one latch door upstairs. I found out from Jack Decatur that it's the same door he had a problem with. Bill or I can shut that door and, miraculously, it will be wide open as soon as we turn our backs. When we first discovered this, Bill insisted that there must be a rational explanation. Finally I dragged him up there and together we did everything we could think of to jiggle that latch loose. We leaned on the door, thumped it, jumped up and down on the floor on either side. Nothing worked. And yet the door does open by itself; it will not stay closed.

"We had another odd experience connected with the bedroom Jack had slept in. My niece, who was about eleven at the time, was staying in that room. She came downstairs, after being up there alone, and claimed that something had been following her around the room. She said it sounded like a small dog; she'd heard the clicking of dog's toenails on the wooden floor. As soon as she stopped, it stopped. She experimented with it, and it followed her into all corners of the room. She's a pretty matter-of-fact kid.

"When a friend got Jack Decatur and me together for the first time last year, we really surprised each other. Neither of us knew that anyone else had experienced strange things in the house. We both felt kind of taken aback—and a little bit frightened—by how similar our descriptions of the older woman were. You get a funny feeling when somebody corroborates a sighting like that; it makes it harder to rationalize or deny.

"I always have a few kids living in the house during the summer. One of my tenants, a young man from New Zealand, came down to the kitchen one morning last week with an odd story. Phil said he'd had a dream, he thought, but it wasn't quite a dream; he said it was too clear, too real. He was confused about what to call this experience.

"He felt somebody yank his covers off in the middle of the night. Then there was silence. He said to himself, 'Well, let's get to it! If you're going to do something, get it over with!' The next thing he knew, he was standing in the middle of his room with the bedside light on. He remembers seeing everything very clearly, almost *too* clearly; his blanket was on the floor at the foot of the bed, his book was where he'd put it down, his clothes were where he'd left them. He remembers how clean, how focused, the image of his room was. He turned his head and saw two figures in the shadows. One of them, a woman with her hair back in a bun, introduced herself as 'Lena.' She referred to the other woman as her sister. As Lena was talking (he can't remember what was said), she was aging, her skin wrinkling; she was turning from a younger to an older woman before his eyes.

"Phil said he didn't remember ever having had a dream that was so lucid, so unnaturally sharp. He'd never heard the name Lena before, and he asked me if it was American.

"Something odd happened to me the other day. I was walking home from work, feeling really tired, just absolutely exhausted. (I've been helping out this summer in a clothing store on Federal Street.) As I walked along the front of the house, I stopped to pick a few of the dead blossoms off my flowers. While I was doing this, I thought to myself, Shall I try the front door, or shall I go around the side? The front door is almost always locked, and I didn't have my key. I just didn't want to go all the way around the building. Thinking, Well, what the heck, I started up the front stairs. I could see that the door was fully closed. When I got near the top step, the door swung open. I thought at first that it was a joke, that one of the kids was hiding behind the door. I had never seen it move in that slow, deliberate way by itself. I stood on the step for a moment, just watching, and then, being really tired, I thumped up the last steps and popped my head in the door. There was no one in sight, and no one anywhere near that part of the house. And, strangely, the bolt on the door was still in the locked position, sticking out from the side.

"What can you say about these weird things that just don't seem possible? The timing was too good. The door had been closed only a moment before, and I didn't hear the grinding sound of the lock being shot back. And besides, if the door had been left unlocked, how did it silently open and present a shot bolt? Let's face it: Something intelligent knew I was tired and opened my door. How nice."

They

"I was twenty-one when Mrs. Deauville hired me. I cleaned her house for one full season, from early May to late September, and then I quit. I couldn't stand it anymore. I was really frightened.

"I was born on Nantucket, and I'm one of those people who's sensitive to anything strange lingering in an old house. I know the moment I walk in the door. As a child, I lived with a visible ghost in a house on the east end of the island, and so the whole idea of spirits has never seemed that odd. I don't welcome that kind of experience, but it has a way of happening to me.

"Mrs. Deauville hired me to clean every week, whether she was there or not. Most of the time the house was empty while I was working. Sometimes she had guests for the weekend, so I'd prepare the house for them and then clean up after they were gone. But she is a meticulous sort of person, and she wanted me to go around and dust and vacuum even if no one had been in the house since the last time I was there.

"On my first day at work, I brought my dog with me. He hopped out of the truck, ran up to the front door, and then wouldn't set foot inside. In all the time I worked there, he would always wait for me in the truck. I tried coaxing him in the front door, and then I tried the back; it was as if there were an invisible line that he wouldn't cross. I couldn't pull him, push him, or carry him inside. He's never done that at any other house.

"When I first stepped in the front door, I remember feeling the hair go up on the back of my neck. I thought to myself, Oh, no. Here we go. There's something here.

"At first they started by doing insignificant, annoying things. They? Yes, I guess I always thought of the source of these goings-on as 'they.' It felt like a group of presences in the house; it never seemed, at least to me, like a single spirit. At any rate, I'd be cleaning, and I'd hear the bleeping signal a phone makes when it's been taken off the hook. I'd put down my dust rag and go downstairs to find that the telephone receiver had been lifted off and laid on its side on the table. I'd hang it back up. Okay, I'd say to myself, I can deal with it.

"I'd be vacuuming, and sometimes I'd hear talking and laughter, the sound of a group of people. I'd shut off the vacuum, and the house would be dead quiet. I'd turn it on, and the voices would start up again. It wasn't an irregular sound in the vacuum motor or anything like that; it was definitely the sound of people conversing, the low and high tones of men and women talking.

"After a few weeks the level of activity began to pick up. I'd be upstairs, and I'd hear furniture being dragged across the floor downstairs. I'd gallop down the stairs and find that a chair had been pulled to the other side of the room or a table dragged into the middle of the floor. I'd say something like, 'Look, I know you don't like me being here, but can you please put up with me for a little while longer? I'm just trying to do my job.' Now, these disturbances only occurred when I was in the house alone, when Mrs. Deauville and her family and guests were nowhere near the place.

"Things got worse. I'd hear the sofa or a sea chest, something really big and heavy, scraping across the floor in the living room, and so I'd hurry down. At first I really wanted to catch them, to see who was doing it and whose voices I was hearing. I wanted, at least, to actually see the furniture being moved. I'd get downstairs, and I'd hear the muffled *thwack! whump!* sound of scatter rugs from upstairs being thrown over the railing behind me. I never did witness these things being done; I'd hear it happening in another part of the house, and find, when I got there, that the objects *had* been moved, but when I arrived at the scene everything was always as still as could be. At that point it was more irritating than frightening; I was trying to straighten out and clean, and they were messing things up as fast as I was putting them in order.

"The house would be worse on some days than on others. I figured I could put up with it as long as it was just silly, bothersome stuff. And I began talking to them the instant they acted up. 'Now stop!' I'd say. 'You're making things awfully difficult for me. This is something I'm being paid to do, you know, and I need to get this done.' It didn't seem to do much good, but it made me feel better.

"One day I went up to the attic, where I'd been cleaning the previous week, and found a really lovely picture right smack in the middle of the floor. It had most definitely not been there before. It was an old photograph of a little girl. She was all dressed up in what looked like her Sunday best. She had long hair in ringlets, a big bow, high ankle shoes that buttoned up the side, and a lovely frilly dress. The picture was in a gorgeous mahogany frame. I'd say it dated back to the early 1900s, maybe the late 1800s.

"I picked up the picture and wondered who the little girl was. I put it on top of one of the boxes in the corner of the attic. I remembered Mrs. Deauville telling me that the house had had quite a bit of family stuff in it when she bought it. She had liked the old furniture and kept most of it around, putting away in the attic the things she didn't care for.

"The next time I came to clean, the picture of the little girl was downstairs on the telephone table. The house had been empty all week. This happened four or five times; I found the picture in the dining room and then in the bedroom. *They* obviously wanted me to see they had moved it.

"When I saw Mrs. Deauville, I mentioned the photograph, just asking her if she knew who the little girl was. She didn't know what I was talking about. I described it in detail. She gave me a strange look, for apparently she had never even seen the photograph. It disappeared shortly after that, again during a week when the house was empty, and I never ran across it again.

"I didn't tell Mrs. Deauville about my crazier experiences in the house; I didn't feel it was my place to tell her that stuff unless she brought it up. And she never did.

"I'd feel more comfortable in some areas of the house than in others.

Certain rooms just seemed to have specific things attached to them. When I was in the downstairs bedroom, I sometimes heard the sound of a horse and carriage coming up the driveway, clear as could be. I think the driveway may have been paving stones at one time, because I'd hear the horses' hoofs, the sounds of their harness creaking and clinking, the grinding of wheels rolling over rock. I'd look out the window as soon as I heard the carriage, but I never saw a thing.

"That downstairs room had a very old-looking mahogany bed. It was short and narrow; perhaps it was a child's bed. It had been in the house when she bought it, Mrs. Deauville told me, and she seemed to feel it was quite valuable. I remember she told me to take special care of it.

"One day I was vacuuming under that bed, and something grabbed the end of my vacuum hose *and held onto it*. I pulled hard, and then the end of the vacuum, the attachment, came right off. It wasn't stuck on anything; I had only been running the vacuum over the bare floorboards. And when I had pulled, it felt like someone was holding on to the other end—you know, there was a slight give to it. When I finally got up my courage to peek under that bed, it all looked as quiet and normal as could be. There was nothing the vacuum could've gotten stuck on, no exposed springs or fabric or anything. It was a good bit later before I dared to reach under there and get the attachment.

"My husband fixed some plumbing in the house, and he noticed a funny thing. He'd take the hoses off the back of the washing machine, during the time it wasn't in use, and put them in the sink. They'd be thrown right out of the sink and onto the floor. This happened over and over. He also felt that same back-of-the-neck prickly sensation I had in the house, and he felt the cold spots. You could walk right into freezing cold areas in any given room; the change in temperature was hard to ignore.

"I mowed the lawn for Mrs. Deauville during the summer. I used a hand mower, and it took quite a long time because there's a good big field out behind the house. I always knew that I was being watched from one of the windows, watched by somebody inside the house. I could feel it. I'd glance up quickly, really expecting to see a face, but I only saw the flat, blank reflection of daylight on glass.

"It was when I started going in twice a week, for shorter periods of time, that it got really bad. I had thought it might be easier to stop in and do three hours at a time instead of staying for a full six.

"It got so that I would unlock the front door and get the strangest feeling. I felt as though the house was too quiet when I stepped inside; it seemed like the place was full of people holding their breath. I got the impression that all sorts of things had been going on and that when I opened the door everyone fell silent.

"Trying to jolly myself out of the feeling, I'd say, 'Hello! I'm here! I'll be as quick as I can!' I didn't have much success.

"Things began to get nasty. The furniture-moving started happening behind my back every ten or twenty minutes. When I was upstairs, I'd hear it happening downstairs, and when I was downstairs I'd hear it happening up. All kinds of things scraped and bumped along over the floor. Objects were never carried, they were always dragged. I remember I ran downstairs once, after an especially noisy session, and found all of the chairs arranged in a tight little circle in the middle of the living room. Another time, while I was in the kitchen, all of the chairs in the outer room were piled up against the back of the kitchen door. Of course I tripped over the chairs and knocked them all over in trying to get out. It was almost like naughty children, but it was also premeditated, deliberate-feeling, and increasingly sinister. Something in the house was trying to get rid of me.

"One day pictures started coming down off the walls. A stack of dishes was moved with a noisy clatter in the kitchen. A rug flew through the air and hit me in the back, and I got whacked by some sofa pillows that zipped halfway across the room on their own. Finally a chair was thrown at me. It missed me and I wasn't hurt, but that did it. I was afraid, really afraid I was going to get injured. My husband urged me to quit, and I did. It was such a relief. They wanted me out of there and, Lord knows, I was happy to go."

The Silk Factory

In 1836, the word was silk; Nantucket's newest industry had the community buzzing. A group of island merchants were promoting the idea that Chinese mulberry trees, and therefore the silkworms they fed, would take naturally to the island's climate and growing conditions. This would make it possible to spin and weave silk locally. It was a daring idea; if it worked, Nantucket would become the first place in America to produce fine silks. Nantucketers have never been afraid to dream, and in the first part of the nineteenth century, with the whaling industry booming, islanders had the cash and the courage to dream large.

On March 31, William H. Gardner, Samuel B. Tuck, and William Coffin founded the Atlantic Silk Company. They had already begun construction on a massive building on Academy Hill, and were in such a hurry that the new building rose sitting on barrels; the foundation didn't go in until the ground thawed in the spring. No one wanted to waste even a week. A great deal of money was spent very quickly. A steam engine, six looms, four spindles, and five hundred bobbins were installed. Cocoons, eggs, silkworms, and Chinese mulberry cuttings arrived, and a man by the name of Gay, an expert in silk manufacture, was lured from Providence to run the factory. Twenty Nantucket women were trained to operate the works. The Atlantic Silk Company boasted ownership of one of the only two power looms in the world.

A report from the Annual Fair of the American Institute, run in the fall of 1836 in New York City, stated the following:

Silk Vesting and Handkerchiefs by the Atlantic Manufacturing Company, Nantucket: articles of superior fabric and manufacture, which, if they could be made to a sufficient extent, would soon sup-plant all silk goods from France or India. Those who have doubts of the practicability of this branch of industry in our country, need dispel their fears, and convince them that it is not only practible [sic], but that it will ere long become one of our staple products. If the good people of Nantucket are as persevering in the silk business as they have been in whaling, their Island will become as celebrated in the annals of silk Manufacture as Lowell is in those of cotton and wool.

It sounded wonderful and hopes were high; apparently the silk produced was competitive, in texture and weave, with the best on the market. However, things went wrong from the start. The mulberry trees did not flourish in Nantucket's sandy soil and cold fogs. Serious internal shenanigans broke the company apart, and local merchants, threatened by this new enterprise, appar-ently contributed to its downfall. By 1844 the factory had closed, having lost many thousands of dollars of its investors' money.

The old factory is a solemn, broad-shouldered structure at the head of Gay Street. At three stories, it towers above the neighboring houses. It was divided vertically into two separate dwelling units by the mid-nineteenth century and then each half was split into small apartments. The east side of the building was used variously as a lodging house and an inn. It has changed hands many times.

Regina Burke bought the east half of the old silk factory in 1978. She ran it as a guesthouse for ten years, living in the basement apartment. She related the following: "My son was born in 1985. When he was just about two and a half, I was lying down with him in my bedroom one afternoon, trying to get him to sleep. We both heard a knocking at the front door. Then the door bumped closed softly, as if someone had entered and then shut it. My son and I both turned toward the open bedroom door. 'Hello?' I called out. There was no answer. Then a tall woman in a dress, a translucent figure, breezed past the bedroom door at a fast walk. You could see through her—she was obviously not flesh and blood—but the outline of her body was distinct. She was in a hurry, and headed for my office in the back. When I'd caught my breath, I got up and followed her. The apartment was empty. My son has never forgotten having seen her; he still asks me about 'that strange lady who came at nap time.'

"There were days when I'd be working in my office, or in the kitchen, which was also toward the back of the apartment, and feel somebody near me. It's hard to explain, but I just knew there was someone watching me. It wasn't frightening, but it was distracting, hard to ignore. It was a very lucid, instinctual perception; although I didn't see anyone, I knew I wasn't alone.

"A year later, I saw the same woman upstairs. It was summer, and I was running around making up the rooms. I turned a corner in the hall, and there she was. We were facing each other, or rather, I was facing her upper torso. She was at least as tall as I. It was a soft, vaporous image, but I could see the hair around her face and her general shape. It seemed to be the same figure that had bustled past my bedroom door. And then, almost instantly, she was gone.

"There's no way of saying for sure which era she belonged to in the building's history, but of course I always wondered about the silk factory. The people who ran it had great determination and will. Perhaps she was checking on the works, just looking in on her weavers, when we met."

Trespassers

"This is the first house we've built, and it's also the first new house we've ever lived in. We finished it in the spring of 1983, and were in by June with our three kids. Kate was six, Nathan was four, and Hunter was just two."

Pam and John Michelsen moved to Nantucket from North Carolina. John was one of the owners of a large restaurant and hotel management company, and came to the island to become managing director of the Sherburne Associates properties. In addition to supervising several smaller businesses, he is responsible for all operations at the Boat Basin, the Harbor House, and the White Elephant. Pam runs her own advertising business out of a studio in their home.

Pam Michelsen is slim, blonde, green-eyed, Southern. It was 6:30 on an unusually hot August evening. Perched on a stool in her kitchen, Pam was absent-mindedly wiping condensation off the sides of her water glass.

"The first thing that happened," she went on, "involved a large can of paint. We had only been in the house a week or so, and I came downstairs with the kids one morning and found a heavy four-gallon can, a great big thing, sitting in the middle of the floor in the den. John came downstairs a few minutes later, and I asked him why he had lugged the can in. He said that he hadn't. The children were so small that they couldn't have picked it up if they'd wanted to. John and I looked at each other. The can was one of several that had been sitting out in the garage. It had not been inside when we went to bed the night before.

"Right from the beginning, the kids heard voices. The boys in particular heard a woman calling their names over and over. I'd be in another room or another part of the house and hear them saying, 'What, Mom? What do you want?' They'd be irritated because I always seemed to be calling them, and I'd be a little irritated because I hadn't said a thing and yet they were continually caterwauling to see what I wanted. It was very peculiar. At first I thought it was just the wind, but it must have happened a hundred times. I remember one afternoon when Nathan came running into the kitchen and said, 'Mom, would you *please* tell Kate to stop calling me?' I had driven Kate over to a friend's house, and I knew Nathan was aware that she wasn't home, so I said something like, 'Nathan, you know Kate isn't home now.' He insisted, 'But Mom, she just keeps calling "Nathan! Nathan! Nathan!" and it's driving me crazy.'

"Our house is built in an 'L' shape, and most of the things that happened went on in the base of the 'L,' so to speak. The garage, the den, and a small bathroom make up the lower section; my studio is situated above.

"One day I was alone in the house with Hunter, who at the time was two and a half, and we were on our way out to do some errands. We went down to the garage and got into the car, and then I ran back upstairs to get my purse and a shopping list. I was up there for a couple of minutes when I heard Hunter's little feet padding up the stairs. I could tell he was hurrying. I turned around as he rushed into the room. His face was drained. He blurted out, 'Mom! The dark shadow went past my window!' I remember thinking how strange it was that he should say such a dramatic thing. He was really too little to be conjuring up spooky stories, and the kids are not allowed to watch unsupervised television. I hadn't heard Kate and Nathan talk about seeing figures or shapes, and Hunter was genuinely scared. Our house is buried in pines, and there's no possibility of a car going by outside and throwing a strange light or reflection inside the garage.

"I picked him up, and we went back down to the car. I must say my heart was really pounding; the can of paint and the woman's voice were odd, but the idea of a dark figure wandering around in the garage was downright terrifying. We looked around the corner, and the garage was empty. I tried to reassure Hunter and myself. Whatever he had seen was gone.

"We didn't harp on this shadow business, not wanting to scare the kids, and they seemed to forget about it pretty quickly. Then a remarkable thing happened.

"I had an old bag of makeup thrown in behind some towels in the back of the linen closet upstairs. It had been there for some time. It was stuff I no longer used, and I was keeping it for St. Paul's Fair or for Halloween. There were lipsticks, eyeliner pencils, and several little compacts with blush. John was at work one Saturday, and I had been out grocery shopping with all three kids. We had locked the house. When we got back, I carried the groceries in to the kitchen and then went to use the bathroom off the den. There, next to the sink, was my bag of makeup. All of the contents had been taken out and neatly arranged in rows on the counter. I couldn't believe my eyes. Neither John nor the kids knew or cared about that old bag of stuff, and besides, the house had been empty all morning. I had taken one of the kids into the bathroom before we left, and the bag of makeup most definitely had not been there.

"John and I had to face the fact that there was something pretty abnormal about our new home. We are not 'ghosty' types, and we have lived in a number of old houses without ever seeing or feeling a thing. Interestingly enough, I think we were more alarmed by these goings-on than the kids were; kids can take a lot in stride, especially at that age.

"The next thing that happened, and that continued to happen frequently over the next two years, involved the entire house. When we leave home, we always put our two dogs down in the basement, then lock the outer doors to the house. At the time that all these weird things were going on, we would return home and find every single light in the house on, all of the outer doors to the house standing wide open, and the dogs outside. We have a long driveway, and our house is hidden from all sides. We know our neighbors, and they wouldn't have been involved in a prank or anything of that kind. At first we thought the house was being broken into, but nothing was ever missing. It was absolutely nuts. This would happen three or four days in a row, and then nothing out of the ordinary would occur for a couple of months.

"There were several times when we had actually locked the dogs into the basement from inside the house. When we got home, the lights were on, the doors open, the dogs out, and *the basement still locked*. It was as if someone had let the dogs out and relocked the basement door behind them.

"During our first year in the house, we went away for a week and left one of John's employees and his wife house-sitting. They are a very straight, 'spade's-a-spade' sort of couple. When we got back, they sat us down and told us that the house had apparently been broken into. They said that on two separate occasions they had locked up everything and gone out, only to return and find doors opened, lights on, and the dogs gone. Each time it happened, they had checked our silver and valuables to see if anything seemed to be missing, but nothing had been disturbed. We told them about our ghost. At first they were incredulous, and then they were quite put out, saying, 'Why on earth didn't you warn us? We were both nervous wrecks!'

"We built our house on an area that had been heavily used by Indians; one finds quartz flakes and broken arrowheads on the dirt roads all through the Dionis area. I can't help wondering if we built on a burial ground, or if we unwittingly disturbed some residue of Indian life. John and I both felt that this presence or visitor in the house was a woman, I guess because of the makeup and the female voice calling the kids. At any rate, it disappeared completely after we had been in the house for maybe two and a half years. Perhaps some ancient spirit felt that we were living someplace we shouldn't be, and just wanted to let us know that we were trespassing."

Tapping

"I was doing some painting for Weather Hill Restoration last February. We were finishing up on a house that was built in 1747. I was told that it had been moved from Sherburne, the earliest settlement on the island, to its present site on the north side of town.

"This particular morning was blustery and gray and wet. I was the first one to get to work. As I was setting up, the electricity went off and on. I thought nothing of it; that's a normal occurrence on a stormy winter day.

"I began to paint. I was working on a window casing in the parlor and listening absent-mindedly to the house creaking and settling in the wind. I felt someone tap me on the right shoulder. Without looking around, I said, 'Hi, Amy,' assuming it was my assistant. No one answered. A moment later, I felt a second and equally firm tapping, again on my right shoulder. It felt like a person patting me with four fingers. It wasn't rough, but it was insistent, and definitely not imagined. 'Amy!' I laughed, 'Is this supposed to be a joke? Quit screwing around! I'm painting.' I hadn't heard her coming in, but between the sounds of the house groaning and the wind howling, it was noisy inside. Still no answer. A second later, someone tapped me again. I twisted around quickly, laughing and a little irritated, and found I was alone. There was no one else in the room. I called out to my assistant. No one answered.

"As I stood there, my mouth probably hanging open, I felt a slight breeze, a very cold movement of air, pass by me from the right. It was icy, much colder than the general room temperature. The latch door to the kitchen was standing all the way open, and the breeze went by me in that direction. And then the kitchen door began to move, and *wham!* clapped shut right before my eyes. Because of the slant of the floor, that particular door has a tendency to swing open on its own. It never swings closed. The rest of the crew didn't arrive for another ten minutes.

"When I left the house that afternoon, I passed a pleasant-looking older woman walking her dog. 'Do you work in that house?' she asked. 'Yes, I do.' 'Did you know that that house has ghosts? It has quite a few. They've been seen by several people.' 'Oh,' I said. I felt the hair going up on the nape of my neck. The woman walked on, and I didn't have the presence of mind to ask her what she was talking about. The moment passed. Maybe that's just as well."

A Trick of the Universe

"What will you have? The rack of lamb is delicious, and the swordfish is always good. I'll have the poached salmon appetizer and the flounder with hollandaise, please, Mary."

Nat Spalding paused to nod hello to several people passing the table. "I come from a Quaker family in Philadelphia. I went to college in Halifax, Nova Scotia, and met a girl who was going to Nantucket for the summer. I followed her, and worked as night watchman and night auditor at this hotel. I taught English and history for four years after graduating, then worked for the Sheraton chain, and then came back here as general manager six years ago.

"When I first came to the hotel, everyone joked about ghosts. I didn't pay much attention to the stories. And then in February of '83, something odd happened. I had a young man, I believe his name was Michael, a pretty down-to-earth fellow, doing renovations on the third floor of the main building. The hotel was closed for the season, and he happened to be working alone up there. I was in the office late one afternoon when he came in with a really funny look on his face. He said, 'I just saw something strange, and I don't know what it was.' He went on to tell me that he had been at the end of the hall on the third floor, near the stair entrance, and looked up to see a ball of light halfway down the hall. Michael described it as a big, glowing mass that was four or five feet in diameter. He stood still, and the ball moved to the left, right through the wall, and disappeared. He didn't stop to investigate but hurried straight down to my office. I can't blame him.

"During the following summer I was told about another odd occurrence. A woman in her thirties and her young daughter, who was eight or nine, were staying in a room on the first floor. The woman called the front desk at about 9:30 P.M. and requested that she be moved. The clerk asked what the problem was, and she said she wasn't sure. The clerk buzzed me, and I went around to her room.

"I knocked on the door. She opened it, said that her daughter was asleep, and asked if we could talk in the hall. We stood just outside her door, and this is what she told me: a small chair in the corner of her room, a Hitchcock, had been hopping up and down by itself. She'd been watching it for at least twenty minutes. The chair was rising three or four inches, as if someone were picking it up, and then sinking slowly to the floor at the same speed. It was going up and down in a rhythmical way, landing with an emphatic *thud* every time it hit. It was also vibrating slightly as it moved.

"You can imagine what was going through my head. Was this woman on drugs? I really scrutinized her, trying to figure out how to take her story. She seemed like a level-headed, calm person. She was sober as could be, and she was serious. I remarked that twenty minutes was a long time, and wasn't she frightened by this strange sight? She said that at first she hadn't quite been able to believe it was happening, and then she had just sat quietly on the bed and tried to figure out what to do. She didn't want to disturb her daughter unless it was absolutely necessary.

"She opened the door, and we looked in. The chair was still. She said that it had stopped moving right after she called the front desk. They had been traveling all day, she explained, and her daughter was really tired. She hated to move her, but didn't see how she herself could relax and go to sleep in the same room with that chair.

"I said, feeling slightly idiotic, 'Yes, of course, I completely understand. We'll find you another room,' and offered to buy her and her daughter dinner the following night to make up for the inconvenience. I sent someone around to help her move.

"We joked about her levitating chair the next day, and she agreed that she had never heard of anything like that ever happening to a 'normal' person. She had a wonderful time on the island, and made reservations for the following summer.

"Now this is pretty crazy—I don't know whether you'd call this a trick of the universe or what—but she and her daughter ended up, the following summer, in the same room. We have dozens of rooms, and the chances of that happening are very slim. I wasn't on duty when they arrived, but I understand it was quite late, and they went right in and unpacked and the little girl went to sleep. The woman was in bed reading when the same chair began, apparently, to move. It started its hopping and jiggling all over again. The woman called the front desk immediately, and she and her daughter switched rooms.

"I think I'd have trouble believing that story if I hadn't actually been involved.

"I had a bizarre experience in the oldest part of the hotel in 1986. There are lots of stories about that section of the building; chambermaids don't like to work there alone because of banging doors and funny noises, and a number of employees have reported odd things over the years. One evening I was showing a young woman who was going to be a summer manager-on-duty what she was expected to do. Her job was to check on everything inside and out before locking up for the night. She had heard some stories about ghosts in the hotel, and I was teasing her. We got up to the top floor, and I said something like, 'Now, if you see a face next to yours in that mirror, you'll know that you are not alone . . . ,' and suddenly one of her earrings was torn right out of her ear. They were big white earrings, costume jewelry. The earring zipped sideways, parallel to the floor, and hit the wall about four feet away. It looked just like someone had jerked it off and thrown it. All I can say is that it defied the laws of gravity; that earring flew horizontally, not down, and it went all by itself. My new manager was out of the building like a shot. She really moved."

Frank Habern:

"It was a specific room in the new addition. The door we had trouble with is on the south side of the building.

"I've been maintenance man at the hotel for six years now. This door business happened in January during my first winter on the job.

"All of the outside doors to that addition are locked with a dead-bolt when the hotel closes. Those dead-bolts are one-and-a-half-inch-wide bars made of iron; this is not like a household lock. Nat and I are the only ones with keys to those particular locks.

"After the holidays I drained the pipes and shut everything down for the winter. Every exterior door was dead-bolted. The doors were replaced a couple of years ago and are in excellent condition.

"The following morning I was driving in to work and noticed that one door was standing open. I hurried over, thinking someone had broken in. When I got there I found that the door didn't seem to have been forced and the room was untouched. The dead-bolt was sticking straight out; it looked like someone had opened the door with a key and then shot the lock back out once the door was wide open. It was pretty odd.

"I called Nat. He didn't know what to make of it either. We checked everything, shrugged, and relocked the room.

"It happened again the following morning. This time it was Nat who found the door open. It was in exactly the same position, with the bolt protruding from the side of the open door.

"On Nat's orders, I reprogrammed the dead-bolt on that particular door so that it required a new key. That night it snowed and snowed, and the following morning the door was open again. Snow had accumulated on the carpeting. And, most interesting, there were no tracks or footsteps anywhere near that door. No one had entered the room from outside.

"Nat and I couldn't believe it. This high-security lock was opening by itself every night, and there were never any signs of a human being having been anywhere in or near the building. Besides that, we knew that there were only two keys in existence and that one was in Nat's pocket and the other in mine.

"This happened for nine or ten days in a row. Nat and I were at a loss; not knowing what else to do, we just closed and rebolted the door every morning.

"And then, just as suddenly as it started, it stopped. The door hasn't opened by itself since."

Jacob Oxford:

"We have a hotel log where all the daily happenings get recorded. My former boss used to come in every morning and read through the previous day's entries, so he knew. After your ghost book came out, he went around to all the employees here and said, 'Make sure you don't tell her *anything*. It's bad for business. People don't want to pay this kind of money and stay in a place where they're worried about being disturbed at night.'

"I've been the night auditor here for ten years now. My shift runs from midnight to 8:00 A.M. After the restaurant and the bar close down, it's usually very quiet, just me and the two cats.

"Shortly after I came to work here, I heard a lot of commotion and a child crying at about 3:00 A.M. A lady ran into the lobby in a skimpy negligee carrying her little girl, who was just three years old. The child was hysterical, and the lady looked pretty scared herself. She had bare feet, and seemed unaware of the fact that she was hardly dressed. She said, 'What happened? What happened?' Everything had been quiet until I heard the child screaming and their hall door slam, so I said, 'What do you mean?' She then told me that they had been sound asleep when there was a horrendous crash on the wall of their room, an unbelievable bang. She said it sounded like a wrecking ball had hit the first floor. She really thought the building was falling down, and claimed that the room was shaking and the furniture rattling. She thought there had either been an earthquake or some terrible explosion.

"I said to the woman, 'Well, let's go back and take a look.' But she refused; she said she'd rather sit in the lobby all night. I had no other room to put her in—the hotel was full—so I got some blankets, and she and her daughter wrapped themselves up and lay down on the couch by the front desk.

"I looked out the back door. There was no one around. Everything on that side of the hotel looked perfectly normal. I examined the wall outside her room, and it looked just like it always does; I saw lines of gray shingles and a window. I closed the door and went up the stairs to the room. When I turned on the light and went in, everything looked just fine. It was nice and quiet.

"The lady and her child stayed in the lobby until morning. No one sleeping on either side of their room or above it complained of hearing anything unusual that night, and yet she and her daughter were awakened by a noise that was so horrendous and so violent that they wouldn't go back in that room until the sun came up.

"The room they were staying in seems to be a bad one; we've had people who've stayed here before call for reservations and ask that they be put anywhere but in that particular room. If you ask them why, they'll laugh and mutter something about not finding the room too comfortable.

"Now prepare yourself; I haven't told you any of the really strange stuff. I hear footsteps regularly. It's always between 3:00 and 3:30 A.M. I can hear them coming down the first-floor corridor, then *thud, thud, thud*, directly across the lobby. Then I hear a door slam right about where the big painting is hanging. I found out recently that there was a door in that wall until 1920 or 1925.

"These steps are firm and sound like they're headed somewhere specific. They always take the same route. The first time I heard them coming, I assumed it was a hotel guest. Then I saw the cats, who were sleeping on one of the armchairs, both lift their heads, all alert, and skitter off like lightning. They aren't afraid of most people, and of course they see a lot of them, but boy, they just streak out of here when they hear those steps coming. Well, when I heard the feet walking across the lobby the first time and I didn't see anyone, I sat pretty still. Then I heard a door close where there wasn't any door. I'm sure I looked kind of bug-eyed that night.

"It did scare me the first few times it happened, but I've since gotten used to it. It's happened hundreds of times over the last ten years. I'll hear it every day for three weeks, and then I won't hear a thing for a couple of months. It goes off and on like that. I don't think there's much pattern to it, although I do seem to hear it more on calm, windless nights. I don't remember noticing it during a bad storm, but then this building is old, and it creaks. A sound has to be good and loud for you to single it out.

"I'm here alone all night, and there isn't much going on, so I sometimes get a little bored. I decided to try talking to the footsteps. One night when I heard them coming I put down my paper and waited until I was sure they were crossing the lobby. Then I said, 'Mr. Ghost! Make yourself known if you're here.' Right away, all the lights went off in the lobby. The switch is at the far end of the room, nowhere near the area where the steps were heard. I couldn't leave the lights out; I got up, feeling pretty shaky, and hurried over to the switch. It had been clicked to the 'off' position. I turned the lights back on. Right in front of my eyes, the switch clicked down again and the lights went off. I said out loud, 'I believe!' and switched the lights back on. They stayed on. And I'll tell you, my heart was pounding.

"Have you ever run across any other stories about a ghost interacting with a living person? It's so crazy-sounding, so unreal, that I really don't talk about it unless I have to. And of course I had no witnesses aside from the cats; these things always happened when I was alone. I don't drink, so alcohol is not a possible explanation.

"A couple of days after the lights-out episode, I was still thinking about it and couldn't quite believe it had happened. I heard the steps coming again, and I guess I was feeling a little cocky, so I challenged him: 'Mr. Ghost! Anybody can flick a switch. What else can you do to show me you're here?' Instantly, I heard the knobs on the cigarette machine being pulled and rattled like wild. It sounded like what you do when you put your money in and nothing comes out; it was a rough, clattery sound. I jumped up from my chair and ran over to the dining room and peeked in. I didn't see anyone, but sure enough, two of the big plastic knobs were twisting and turning on their own. There was absolutely no way I could be seeing what I was seeing.

"I must have said, 'Wow' out loud, and just then the recessed ceiling lights in the dining room all went out. Those lights are supposed to be on all night, I guess for security reasons, and the switch is quite a distance from the dining room door. Trying to sound calm, I said, 'Yes, I can tell you're here,' and thought to myself, Well, Jacob, now you've done it. Without allowing myself to pause, I kind of dove into the darkness and groped my way along, feeling for the plants and chairs, until I got to the light switch. God knows where I found the courage.

"The switch was *down*. Again, it had been physically clicked to the 'off' position. I turned the lights back on, and they stayed that way for the rest of the night.

"I spoke to the ghost on one other occasion. You know, you go over and over these experiences in your mind, and after a while you can hardly believe they were real. I guess I just wanted to see, once more, if the ghost would do something. I heard the steps coming, and when they got to the middle of the lobby I asked them again to give me some proof. Right away, one of the doors into the kitchen began to swing wildly. The other door stayed still. The door that was swinging moved so violently that it covered a full 180-degree path. It went all the way back in the kitchen, all the way open in the dining room.

"That was the last time I talked to Mr. Ghost. I knew, then, that he could exert an impressive physical strength and that he could hear me. That was enough. I've thought about asking him to show himself, but I don't want to push the whole thing too far. I'm not sure I want to get any more involved with this spirit or hobgoblin or lost soul or whatever he is.

"Four or five years ago, we had a young English boy working as a dishwasher in the kitchen. Near the end of the night, he came bursting suddenly through the swinging doors. He had some hairnet contraption on his head and was soaking wet and messy from a night of work. He ran through the dining room, between tables where people were sitting, and right on through the lobby and out the front door. He called later to say that he wasn't returning, and I don't believe he ever set foot in the building again. He told me months later, when I saw him on the street, that he had been working at the sink and had seen a tall, misty form moving toward him across the kitchen. He said it came directly at him, and that as it was closing in he felt a dreadful coldness. It was then that he took off. He began to shake just telling me about it. He's a regular guy, a nice boy. He was very upset by that experience."

Tim Strauss:

"I'm a musician, and I've been playing at the hotel for ten years now. I know this place very well. I used to stay on the first floor in early spring and in late fall when the employee dorms were too cold to use.

"I was the only one in the building at night. We had a few carpenters on board doing renovation and wallpapering, but they would leave at five. The hotel was closed, and there was no reason for Jacob to be there in the off season.

"Late at night I would hear people walking. I heard footsteps right over me, on the second floor. Footsteps, not just creaks: they were the sounds of people moving around in their room. I also heard walking in the first-floor corridor, and doors slamming as people went in and out. A couple of times I stuck my head out the door and looked up and down the hallway, but I never saw anything. The building just seemed to have a life of its own."

George Hentz:

"I'm in charge of reservations for the hotel. Back in the winter of 1978 or '79 I used to take turns house-sitting the main building with Dominic Gale, who was then the manager. I stayed in a room off that first-floor corridor.

"At night I'd check everything, lock up the hotel, and go to bed. Sometimes I heard doors opening and closing. I'd listen carefully to see if it might be someone trying to get in from outside, but it was not. It was the sound of doors inside the building.

"It didn't exactly frighten me, but I didn't investigate, either. I just pulled up the covers and said, 'Well, interesting,' to myself and went to sleep.

"I commented on it to Dominic one day, and he acknowledged that he'd heard the same noises. It's a creaky old building, but what I heard was definitely the sound of human activity. The doors were all shut and locked in the morning, just as they had been the night before."

Tony Wenzell:

"I'm now assistant controller for the hotel. Ten years ago, I was out here for the summer, and I worked one night a week as night auditor.

"I still can't explain this at all, and I probably wouldn't trust my own memory if I hadn't talked with other people working in the building.

"Once in a while I'd hear someone at the other end of the lobby. I'd hear the fire doors, which are big, heavy panels separating the first-floor corridor from the lobby, being opened and then closed. I'd been told to shut those doors at night, and I always did, although I found out later that they are only there for emergencies. Those doors absolutely do not open on their own, as some doors do with a draft; they are built to withstand stress and heat, and you have to pull hard to get them open.

"So, I'd hear the doors open, and then I'd hear someone walking into the lobby, and then a door banging, and then silence. The first couple of times I heard this, I craned my neck out, leaning over the front desk to see if anyone was at that end of the room. I didn't see anybody. *O-kaay*, I said to myself, and went back to what I was doing. I didn't get up.

"I can't tell you exactly when this happened, but it was always sometime between 2:00 and 4:00 A.M. I'd already heard the noises during several different shifts when once, on hearing the fire doors open, I happened to look into the big mirror that hangs across from the front desk.

"This is impossible, but instead of my own reflection I saw the entrance to the first-floor hallway. It's crazy, because that entrance is thirty feet away from the front desk. And I saw something else. There was an extremely tall man standing in front of the fire doors.

"He was nebulous, he wasn't solid, but I could see that he was at least six-foot-three or six-foot-four and that he was wearing a long dark overcoat of some kind and a dark, wide-brimmed hat. His clothing didn't look contemporary. He was facing out toward the lobby, and his face was partially hidden by that hat.

"I was shocked. By the time I realized something really bizarre was going on, the image was gone and I was staring, horrified, at the reflection of my own face and the front desk. I dismissed that experience as being some sort of nutty time warp or delusion. I knew the building was old, and I knew I had seen something that did not belong to the present.

"Several weeks later, I was standing in front of the desk when I heard the fire doors opening. I walked on down there to take a look. And there he was. The image lasted for maybe ten seconds. It was the same man, standing at the hall entrance, looking tall and dark and pretty grim.

"After that, when I heard the fire doors opening at that hour and steps thudding into the lobby, I didn't look up at the mirror. I didn't look out across the lobby. I'd take a deep breath, sit very still, and try to think about something else."

The End of September

"This is the bedroom. It does have the strangest door; a large man has to squeeze through like a crab, sideways and head down, to fit. But once you're in, the room opens up into a warm, sunny square. Yes, the floorboards in this house are all original. They are such different widths and lengths that they form, within each room, a kind of splintery crazy quilt. They must have been treated with untold buckets of oil, but I don't believe they've ever been sanded down or refinished. The door panels, the corner posts, the overhead beams, and most of the windows look just as they did when the builder put them in place two and a half centuries ago. As a matter of fact, I've been having a heck of a time this week trying to get ancient putty out of this window frame. When one of those eighteenth-century builders did a job, he did it to last.

"This is my office over here. Have a seat. I'm not quite sure where to begin. I haven't told anyone but my wife about these experiences, and wasn't planning to until I heard you give a talk at Rotary the other day.

"Mary and I moved into this house three years ago this summer. Mary is a native Nantucketer, and I've been here since 1983. We met on the island. I'm an architect; I came to Nantucket to work for Design Associates, and I now have my own business.

"Mary and I slept, when we were first in the house, in that front bedroom. One night I was awakened from a sound sleep by the bed shaking. It was enough of a motion to make me open my eyes and look for Mary, who I thought might be getting up. But no, she was as still as a stone, curled up next to me in a deep sleep. And then, out of the corner of my eye, I saw someone at the foot of the bed. It was a woman.

"The people across the street leave their outside lights on all night, so it was dim but not completely dark in our room. The woman was facing me, standing at my side of the end of the bed. She was shimmery, opaque. Now, this sounds really strange, but she was wind-blown. She looked as if she were standing in a stiff breeze. Strands of dark, shoulder-length hair moved around her face. Her gown was long and white, and had tiers of ruffles on it. I can remember that it seemed to fit snugly under her chin.

"I was awake, or at least I sure felt that I was, and I really wasn't afraid. I had a strangely immobilized feeling, as if I couldn't even reach out to wake Mary. I just lay there looking at the woman. I couldn't see her features in any great detail, but if I had to describe her expression, I'd say she looked like a mother who has come to check on a sleeping child. She was a youngish woman, not terribly tall; she might have been just over five feet.

"It's hard to say how long I looked at her. Ten seconds? Twenty seconds? And then, without changing position, she floated backward, still looking toward me, and out the open door.

"Oddly enough, I felt calm about the experience, and after a short while I drifted off to sleep again. It wasn't until the next morning, when I told Mary about what had happened, that I realized how wacky and scary it sounded.

"This happened toward the end of September. The following year, at around the same time, exactly the same thing occurred. I was awakened from a deep sleep and found myself facing this woman. Again, her hair and dress were moving in a wind I couldn't feel, and after several seconds she floated silently out the door.

"We moved into the downstairs bedroom the following year. I thought to myself, Well, I guess that'll be the last of her. But when the end of September came around, the experience was repeated downstairs. Again, after standing at the foot of the bed for several seconds, the woman drifted backward and out the door. Mary was horrified by the idea of the first two visits, so I never even told her about the last one. They really don't frighten me; I never feel as though this woman means me any harm.

"You might want to speak to the Eastons, the owners of the house. I wonder if anyone in their family ever saw the woman or if they know who she is. I've never said anything to them. I guess it's a little embarrassing to talk about nocturnal visitations from a ghostly female. But go ahead and give them a call, and I'll let you know if I see my friend again in September."

Jane Easton:
"Well, that's very interesting. We lived in the house for fifteen years. As you know, it's a very old building. I was made aware of two presences in the house over the years, but I don't know anything about a young woman.

"My first experience was with a little girl. This happened at night in the front bedroom upstairs. My husband and I were sleeping, and I felt the corner of the bed go down on my side. It felt as though a young child had sat down. I couldn't see anything, but I had an immediate and very strong impression that this was a little girl of about three and that her name was Annie. I felt I had to say something to her, a soothing word, I suppose, and I said something innocuous, like, 'Are you all right?' I felt the child get up as I spoke, and then she was gone.

"I thought that maybe I had imagined this until a guest of ours, also a woman, reported the same experience after sleeping in the front bedroom. She came down in the morning and told me that she was sure she had been visited by a little girl. Her sense of what had happened was very similar to mine.

"Another odd thing occurred at night in that house. I remember it was early fall, maybe September or October. I walked into the kitchen, where we have a huge eighteenth-century hearth. The lights were off, but there was enough light coming in from the next room to see. I was just going in to pick up a magazine that I'd left on the kitchen table.

"There, standing in front of the hearth, was a figure. It was vaporous, kind of cloudy, but was definitely a human form. It had a shawl over its head and back. I guess I froze. I remember wondering if the form was a woman or a man, and then it was gone.

"I saw that figure twice, so I know it wasn't just some trick of lighting. These old Nantucket houses have been used by many people, and I guess it shouldn't seem strange that we occasionally experience something that is out of the ordinary. It seems to me that we still have a lot to learn about the workings of the human spirit."